C000023698

First Print Edition [1.0] -1440h

Copyright © 1440 H./2018 C.E.
Taalib al-Ilm Educational Resources

http://taalib.com
Learn Islaam, Live Islaam.^{SM}

ISBN EAN-13:   978-1-938117-65-7   [Soft cover Print Edition]

GOLDEN WORDS UPON GOLDEN WORDS…FOR EVERY MUSLIM.

"Imaam al-Barbahaaree, may Allaah have mercy upon him said:

May Allaah have mercy upon you! Examine carefully the speech of everyone you hear from in your time particularly. So do not act in haste and do not enter into anything from it until you ask and see: Did any of the Companions of the Prophet, may Allaah's praise and salutations be upon him, speak about it, or did any of the scholars? So if you find a narration from them about it, cling to it, do not go beyond it for anything and do not give precedence to anything over it and thus fall into the Fire.

Explanation by Sheikh Saaleh al-Fauzaan, may Allaah preserve him:

'Do not be hasty in accepting as correct what you may hear from the people especially in these later times. As now there are many who speak about so many various matters, issuing rulings and ascribing to themselves both knowledge and the right to speak. This is especially the case after the emergence and spread of new modern day media technologies.

Such that everyone now can speak and bring forth that which is in truth worthless; by this meaning words of no true value - speaking about whatever they wish in the name of knowledge and in the name of the religion of Islaam. It has even reached the point that you find the people of misguidance and the members of the various groups of misguidance and deviance from the religion speaking as well. Such individuals have now become those who speak in the name of the religion of Islaam through means such as the various satellite television channels. Therefore be very cautious!

It is upon you oh Muslim, and upon you oh student of knowledge individually, to verify matters and not rush to embrace everything and anything you may hear. It is upon you to verify the truth of what you hear, asking, 'Who else also makes this same statement or claim?', 'Where did this thought or concept originate or come from?', 'Who is its reference or source authority?'. Asking what are the evidences which support it from within the Book and the Sunnah? And inquiring where has the individual who is putting this forth studied and taken his knowledge from? From who has he studied the knowledge of Islaam?

Each of these matters requires verification through inquiry and investigation, especially in the present age and time. As it is not every speaker who should rightly be considered a source of knowledge, even if he is well spoken and eloquent, and can manipulate words captivating his listeners. Do not be taken in and accept him until you are aware of the degree and scope of what he possesses of knowledge and understanding. As perhaps someone's words may be few, but possess true understanding, and perhaps another will have a great deal of speech yet he is actually ignorant to such a degree that he doesn't actually posses anything of true understanding. Rather he only has the ability to enchant with his speech so that the people are deceived. Yet he puts forth the perception that he is a scholar, that he is someone of true understanding and comprehension, that he is a capable thinker, and so forth. Through such means and ways he is able to deceive and beguile the people, taking them away from the way of truth.

Therefore what is to be given true consideration is not the amount of the speech put forth or that one can extensively discuss a subject. Rather the criterion that is to be given consideration is what that speech contains within it of sound authentic knowledge, what it contains of the established and transmitted principles of Islaam. As perhaps a short or brief statement which is connected to or has a foundation in the established principles can be of greater benefit than a great deal of speech which simply rambles on, and through hearing you don't actually receive very much benefit from.

This is the reality which is present in our time; one sees a tremendous amount of speech which only possesses within it a small amount of actual knowledge. We see the presence of many speakers yet few people of true understanding and comprehension.' ”

[The eminent major scholar Sheikh Saaleh al-Fauzaan, may Allaah preserve him- 'A Valued Gift for the Reader Of Comments Upon the Book Sharh as-Sunnah', page 102-103]

This pocket edition is based upon appendices taken from the larger book:

30 Days of Guidance: Signposts Towards Rectification & Repentance

A Short Journey through Selected Questions & Answers with Sheikh Muhammad Ibn Saaleh al-'Utheimeen

[Book 3- 30 Days of Guidance Series]

The original course book is intended for any Muslim who wishes to improve his life and rectify his heart. Yet this self rectification or purification of the soul must be done in the correct way and upon the correct foundation of knowledge from the Sunnah, if it is to lead to true success in both this life and the next.

Ibn al-Qayyim, may Allaah have mercy upon him, also stated, 'The true purification of the soul and the self is directly connected to those messengers sent to humanity..."

It discusses in detail the inward and outward changes and steps we must take as striving Muslims to improve and bring our lives into a better state after mistakes, sins, slips, and negligence. Discussing real life problems and issues faced by Muslim of all ages and situations -the Sheikh advises and indicates the road to reform, repentance, and true rectification.

Collected and Translated
by Abu Sukhailah Khalil Ibn-Abelahyi al-Amreekee

[Available: **Now**] pages: **370+**
price: (Soft cover) **$27.5**
(Hard cover) **$45**
(eBook) **$9.99**

BENEFITS OF TAQWA, FRUITS OF TRUE BELIEFS, HIGH GOALS AND ASPIRATIONS, & MODERN MEDIA

LET THE SCHOLARS SPEAK- CLARITY & GUIDANCE (BOOK 3)

Translated & Compiled By
Abu Sukhailah Khalil Ibn-Abelahyi

Table of Contents

AMENDED INTRODUCTION

In the name of Allaah, The Most Gracious, The Most Merciful
Verily, all praise is due to Allaah, we praise Him, we seek
His assistance and we ask for His forgiveness. We seek
refuge in Him from the evils of our souls and the evils of
our actions. Whoever Allaah guides, no one can lead him
astray and whoever is caused to go astray, there is no one
that can guide him. I bear witness that there is no deity
worthy of worship except Allaah alone with no partners.
And I bear witness that Muhammad is His worshipper
and Messenger.

 *❖ Oh you who believe, fear Allaah as He ought to
be feared and do not die except while you are Muslims.
❖*-(Surah Aal-'Imraan:102)

 *❖ Oh mankind, fear Allaah who created you from a
single soul and from that, He created its mate. And from them
He brought forth many men and women. And fear Allaah to
whom you demand your mutual rights. Verily, Allaah is an
ever All-Watcher over you.❖*-(Surah an-Nisaa:1)

 *❖ Oh you who believe, fear Allaah and speak a word
that is truthful (and to the point) - He will rectify your deeds
and forgive you your sins. And whoever obeys Allaah and
His Messenger has achieved a great success.❖*-(Surah al-
Ahzaab:70-71)

As for what follows:

Al-Imaam Ibn al-Qayyim, may Allaah the Most High have mercy upon him, one of the well known scholars who has several works related to self rectification upon the pure Sunnah, said, [1]

> *"Every single individual from among the people has a rich bounty in their very life which they must be aware of and realize that it is in fact possible to exchange it for and purchase with it a treasure from the treasures which do not end, whose blessings continue on and on never ceasing.*
>
> *However, so many people lose out and waste this bounty of life. Or even worse, they take this tremendous bounty of life and exchange it and spend it for that which will only lead to their own eventual destruction and their own severe loss! This is despite that being something which no one with any sense would knowingly permit to happen, except for the most ignorant and foolish of people, those lacking in any good understanding at all.*
>
> *But, without question, this severe ruin and their loss will eventually be made apparent and plain to him on that final day of mutual loss, as Allaah says,* ❀**On the Day when every person will be confronted with all the good he has done, and all the evil he has done, he will wish that there were a great distance between him and his evil. And Allaah warns you against Himself (His Punishment) and Allaah is full of Kindness to the (His) slaves.**❀*-(Surah Aal-Imraan: 30)*

He, may Allaah the Most High have mercy upon him, explains that the Messenger of Allaah, may the praise and salutations of Allaah be upon him, taught his Ummah that

---

[1]   Ighaathatul-Lahfaan, pg. 89

being successful in this life means first purifying our hearts and actions by opposing our desires and truly calling our souls to account as to how we are living as Muslims ,

> *"...What is intended here is the mentioning of the cure for the ailment of the heart by the individual taking control over it and what it constantly urges and incites towards, and this has two specific cures:*
>
> *Firstly, calling of the heart to account through self-examination and, secondly, opposing its desires. As the destruction of one's heart is caused by heedlessness and inattention towards self-examination as well as one's simply conforming to and following its desires.*
>
> *In a hadeeth narrated by Imaam Ahmad and others on the authority of Shadaad Ibn Aws, who said: The Messenger of Allaah, may Allaah's praise and salutations be upon him, said,* **{The intelligent person is the one who takes command over his soul and strives for what will come after death. And the incompetent person is the one who simply follows his desires and merely hopes for Allaah's mercy.}** *Taking command here means calling his soul to account through self-scrutiny and accounting...."*

Rectification of our lives through proper self accounting leads to us consider in detail how we use the different blessing which Allaah has given us each individually. al-Wazeer Ibn Habeerah, may Allaah have mercy upon him, from the earlier generations reminds us in a couplet of poetry of the value of using the blessing of time in our lives correctly, [2]

> *One's time is from the most precious of things one can struggle to preserve*
>
> *Yet, I see it is from among the easiest of things to waste and lose.*

[2]   Dheel Tabaqaat al-Hanaabilah vol. 1 pg. 281

Likewise Sheikh 'Abdur-Rahman as-Sa'dee, may Allaah have mercy upon him, reminds us in the following lines of poetry of the direct consequences of how we use our lives and blessings,[3]

The one who thanks Allaah with the actions of his heart, tongue, and his deeds,

should have glad tidings that Allaah will increase him in His favors.

Whereas the one who treats those blessings with heedlessness by only entering

into the disobedience of Allaah, only moves himself towards a severe punishment.

With the many ideas around us today, many of us as Muslims have this question *"How should I best be spending my life?"* And this is an important question for anyone truly seeking success in this life. The general answer and guidance of our beloved Prophet is simple and complete. It applies to us as individual Muslims, just as it does to us as part of an Ummah of well over a billion and a half individuals. The guiding scholar Sheikh Bakr Abu Zayd, may Allaah have mercy upon him, mentioned and explain that clear answer and guidance the Prophet gave when asked,[4]

"...And as found in Saheeh Muslim and others, A man requested that the Prophet, may Allaah's praise and salutations be upon him, advise him. The Messenger, upon him be Allaah's praise and salutations, said to him, **{Say: I believe in Allaah and then be upright and steadfast.}**

So he has combined for him in his words **{Say: I believe in Allaah...}** : *that which carries the meaning of rectifying one's beliefs. And encompassed within his words* **{...then be upright and steadfast.}**: *that which carries*

[3]   As narrated in 'Small Beneficial Portions From The Statements Of The Guiding Scholar Sheikh 'Abdur-Rahman Ibn Naasir as-Sa'dee

[4]   Hukm Al-Intimaa' by Sheikh Bakr Abu Zayd: pg. 13

the meaning of rectifying one's deeds and actions.

And upon the rectification of these two matters is the route to truly establish the Muslim Ummah."

Yet many people are confused as to what the uprightness referred to here is. We live in an age in which many, including Muslims, are unclear as to what standing upon the truth means.

They may ask themselves, *"How do I know what is actually right and wrong?"* This important question, and the common confusion surrounding it, is one which affects each and every one of our lives and those of our children, as we are faced with decisions related to it every single day. For if we do not fully understand what is good and bad, how can we possibly practice it? The extraordinary scholar Ibn Rajab, may Allaah have mercy upon him, in his work 'Jaame'a al-Uloom wa al-Hukm' discussed this dilemma of first struggling to understand what is right and wrong, as related to the obligation of enjoining what is right and forbidding what is wrong.

He showed that the first generations considered it a more serious and significant danger for a Muslim to not clearly know and broadly understand the true criterion and clear standard of right and wrong. Within his explanation of the thirty-fourth hadeeth, the well known authentic hadeeth narration found in Saheeh Muslim about changing wrongdoing, under the heading *"Prohibiting Wrongdoing And Evil Is From Emaan"* he narrates, [5]

"...Ibn Mas'ood heard a man saying 'Destroyed or ruined is the one who does not enjoin what is good and does not forbid what is wrong.' Ibn Mas'ood said to him in response, **"Destroyed or ruined is the one who does not comprehend with his heart what is good and what is wrong."** [6]

[5]   Jaame'a al-Uloom wa al-Hukm vol. 2 pg. 245
[6]   The general wording mentioned by Ibn Rajab is found in the narration of

This indicates that understanding and comprehending what is good and evil with one's heart is an individual obligation which is not ever removed from any Muslim. Since the one who does not comprehend it is someone personally ruined and destroyed, whereas forbidding and preventing it with one's tongue and with one's hand, in relation to others, is something which is only to be carried out according the specifics of one's capability and circumstances. "

...these hadeeth narrations [7] together indicate the conditional obligation of comprehensively forbidding wrong and wrongdoing according to the ability one possesses.

As for the more limited forbidding and censuring of it within one's own heart, then this is always required. Such that someone not forbidding and censuring wrong and wrongdoing in his heart indicates that emaan or faith in Allaah has completely left his heart....

As such we must always strive to first understand what is right and wrong as Muslims, and this can only be done through accepting the full revelation of the Noble Qur'aan and the Sharee'ah guidance which Allaah sent down to guide us. This is a fact repeatedly mentioned in the Qur'aan itself in many verses which we hear and recite in our daily prayers. Yet many Muslims without realizing it often proceed through their lives with only a generally weak understanding of the clear beliefs and practical

transmitted in Shu'ab-al-Emaan no. 7588. The wording of the narrations in the Musannaf of Ibn Abee Shaybaah narration number 40188 -vol 7. pg. 504 states, "On the authority of Ibn Masood, he was asked is the one who does not enjoin what is good and does not forbid what is wrong ruined? He replied, "No, but ruined is the one who does not comprehend with his heart what is good and does not censure or condemn with his heart what is wrong and wrongdoing."

[7]   A similar narration has been narrated by Imaam at-Tabaraanee in his work Mua'jam al-Kabeer narration number 8564 and the hadeeth scholar al-Haythamee mentioned it in his work al-Majmu'a az-Zawaid vol. 7, pg. 257 stating 'Its narrators are all the reliable narrators of Saheeh al-Bukhaaree.'

Sharee'ah knowledge needed to make their lives, inwardly and outwardly, truly successful and fulfilled. They do not have all the knowledge needed to be successful when their lives are finally accounted for.

This issue of understanding right and wrong according to Islaam is directly connected to our individual personal identity and whether it is foremost as a Muslim who has submitted to Allaah and His perfected preserved religion and who first turns to gain knowledge of its guidance rather than unevidenced opinions and the unrestricted following of our culture, or blind following of what our father believed and proceeded upon. The guiding scholar Sheikh Zayd Ibn Muhammad al-Madkhalee, may Allaah the Most High, have mercy upon him, said, [8]

> *"How significant is the need of the Muslim Ummah in this age and time for earnestly and diligently seeking Sharee'ah knowledge, regardless of whether they believe this to be something difficult for them. As there is nothing within the endeavor of seeking knowledge which is truly expensive or too costly, since in truth everything is made easier through the seeking of Sharee'ah knowledge, being diligent in gaining it and spreading it. As this knowledge is life, and without it one will not find that blessed good life.*

> *The intelligent and perceptive Muslim is the one who feels and recognizes his need for this Sharee'ah knowledge. And so he learns and studies, such that he is continually and constantly desiring to listen to knowledge, read knowledge, and spread and share knowledge. Know that such a Muslim stands upon engaging in worship of Allaah from the initial time that he places his feet down, or gets into that vehicle which he takes, in order to gain and gather Sharee'ah knowledge.*

[8]   As found in his explanation of al-Adab al-Mufrad: volume 3 pg. 113

Just as many people today are often distracted and overly occupied with social media updates on their phones, some of the past scholars were absorbed and constantly occupied with beneficial knowledge. The well known scholar in the sciences of Arabic grammar Muhammad Ibn Ahmad Abu Bakr al-Kheyaat al-Baghdaadee, [9]

> "...would study constantly most of his time even while travelling in the streets. He would sometimes trip on a step or his animal would bump into something while he was reading!"

Every person in this life has priorities and a focus they proceed upon, but as Muslims we must always ask, what does Allaah actually want for ours to be? We should each have a commitment to steadily gaining an essential foundation of knowledge according to our ability and circumstances that allows us to truly understand what Allaah wants from us. As beneficial knowledge gained sincerely for Allaah's sake opens the door for us to truly and properly implement and obey Allaah's commands and stay away from His prohibitions, thus having taqwa in our lives as we struggle to live Islaam. The guiding scholar Sheikh Ibn Baaz, may Allaah have mercy upon him, reminds us that this taqwa is in fact the cause of gaining every form of good, personally and collectively, [10]

> "Understand also that this religion of Islaam gathers within it every type and form of good for you. Such that the one who establishes themselves upon the guidance of Islaam, implements its guidelines, properly performs its duties, and struggles against himself to realize its guidance, this one becomes someone who properly has taqwa of Allaah.

---

[9]   al-Hayth Alaa Talaba Ilm wa al-Ijtihaad fee Jamehee" of Abu Hilaal al-'Askaree pg. 77
[10] Selections from an article at the website of the Sheikh http://binbaz.org.sa/ article/361

He is someone promised the reward of entrance into Jannah and the blessing of Allaah's different favors in the Hereafter. He is the person who is promised a life that is untroubled by many types of worry and stress and whose general affairs are made easy for him.

He is the one promised forgiveness for the sins which he commits as well as his sins of neglect or omission. He is the one who is promised victory over the opponents of the Muslims, and protection from their plans and schemes, all if he establishes himself upon the religion of Allaah, proceeds patiently, struggles with himself for Allaah's sake, and gives both Allaah His essential rights and the created beings their rights.

This is the one having taqwa, the one who is a believer in Islaam, the one upon doing good, the one who has been successful, the one who has been guided by Allaah and is righteous. This is the one who has taqwa of Allaah, the Most Glorified and the Most Exalted, and is the true Muslim...

...I say clearly that every person who carefully considers and contemplates those selections related to having taqwa or fear of Allaah which are found in the Book of Allaah, the Most Glorified and the Most Exalted, and as found in the Sunnah of His Messenger Muhammad, upon him be Allaah's praise and salutations, they will come to understand that having taqwa is in fact the actual cause of gaining every form of good, both in this worldly life and in the Hereafter.

Certainly, if you, oh worshiper of Allaah, read the Book of your Lord from the beginning to the end, you will discover that taqwa is the source of every form of possible goodness, the key to receiving every form of good, and the reason leading to obtaining every form of good in both the life of this world and in the life of the Hereafter.

Similarly, trials, ordeals, difficulties, and punishments only reach us and emerge through our own negligence and carelessness in our efforts of having taqwa, or through being neglectful of one or more aspects of having taqwa. As taqwa is the primary cause leading to our contentment and success, and keeping away from various worries and forms of stress. It is what leads to our honor and victory in this worldly life and the life of the Hereafter...

....The religion of Islaam has been called 'birr', as through practicing it every type of well-being is achieved. And the religion of Islaam has been called 'guidance', as the one who establishes himself upon its way becomes guided towards goodness of character and goodness of deeds. This is since Allaah sent His Prophet , may Allaah's praise and salutations be upon him, to perfect the beneficial character, and to bring about the having of good and sound actions and deeds. Just as is mentioned in the hadeeth narration where the Prophet , may Allaah's praise and salutations be upon him, said, **{I was sent to perfect good character.}**

Likewise in the narration of Unais the brother of Abu Dhar, may Allaah be pleased with him, who after he returned from Mecca told Abu Dhar that he saw the Messenger of Allaah inviting to excellent character. [11]

For this reason this religion has been called guidance, as it guides the person who establishes himself upon it towards goodness of character and goodness of deeds. Just as Allaah, the Most Glorified and the Most Exalted, said: **...whereas there has surely come to them the Guidance from their Lord!**-(Surah an-Najm:

---

[11] Saheeh al-Bukhaaree 3861, and Saheeh Muslim 2474

23) And Allaah the Most High said: ❦**They are on (true) guidance from their Lord, and they are the successful.** ❧*-(Surah al-Baqarah: 5) And Allaah the Most High said:* ❦**.... and it is they who are the guided ones.**❧*-(Surah al-Baqarah:157).*

It is through consideration of all of this that we come to understand the full meanings of these different expressions and terms: 'al-Islaam,' 'al-emaan', 'at-taqwa,' 'al-hudaa,' 'al-birr,' 'al-ibaadah,' and others related to them..."

THE TRUE WAY OF THE PEOPLE OF THE SUNNAH TAKES EVERY OBEDIENCE FROM THE SUNNAH

The Sunnah, both generally and specifically, contains the guidance and guidelines needed to obey Allaah, strive to be righteous, and be successful in our lives. Yet in our age there is a great deal of discussion and differing as to what is the proper way to bring about the rectification of both the individual and society. Many people unknowingly have formed and simply followed their own opinions, personal perceptions, and ideas. But, by Allaah's mercy, the steadfast scholars upon the Sunnah have always called to and clarified the correct answer to this, as it is a central part of the methodology which Allaah gave the prophets and messengers. Ibn al-Qayyim said, making clear both the problem and the solution in his work al-Madaarij as-Saalikeen,[12]

"The true purification of the soul and the self is directly connected to those messengers sent to humanity. Certainly Allaah sent messengers for the purpose of this purification of souls, and commanded them to pursue this, and brought it about through their hands, through

[12] al-Madaarij as-Saalikeen vol 2. pg. 356

efforts of calling, teaching, and guiding the people. They were sent to guide the various nations of the earth. Moreover the purification of the souls is something more difficult than curing diseases of the body, as the ailments specific to the soul are more severe.

As such, anyone who works to purify his soul through some methods of devised physical movements and contrived practices of speech and words, or through ways of seclusion from the people which the messengers of Allaah never came with, then he is like a person who seeks to cure a disease by following his mere opinion about treatment of an bodily illness. Yet how could he follow his personal opinion compared to the established knowledge of a knowledgeable physician??!

As such, the messengers of Allaah are the true doctors for the ailments of the hearts. There is no path to truly cure and rectify the hearts except by means of their revealed paths, through their hands as messengers, and through purely surrendering to and complying with their guidance. And we seek Allaah's assistance in our affairs."

Among the paths of misguidance prevalent today in Muslim lands, as well as in Muslim communities in the West, is a renewed call to adopt one of the many paths of Sufism developed after the age of the Companions of the Messenger of Allaah. This way of Sufism is called to as the best road to purify our hearts and souls as Muslims. Yet there are other Muslims who instead look towards how the first generations of Muslims, starting with the Companions, purified their hearts. Those who follow the Salaf oppose the call to this methodology of new methods developed by the various Sufee orders. They do not accept these many different new practices of self-purification through innovated and altered acts of remembrances, nor do they accept many of the distorted beliefs behind them.

What this, at times, leads to is that when some Muslims are asked about the efforts of those Muslims who follow the way of the first three generations, some of them say, *"Those Salafees continually talk about beliefs, as if there were no other parts of Islaam!!"*. This leads others, from among the general Muslims, to wrongly accept this false claim from them due to their lack of knowledge of what the Salafee scholars, past and present, have always taught and called to. If they shut their eyes and ears to the words of the Salafee scholars, they might be able to falsely believe that the way of the Salaf, and those committed to following Islaam as they did, does not consider self purification and character development as a truly important priority for Muslims.

But in fact, the scholars upon the way of the Salaf throughout the centuries have always given importance to character, good behavior, self purification, and affirmed every form of general worship, inward and outward, which is pleasing to Allaah. We find within the books of those scholars who followed and called to the way of the first generations, that they advance a complete and balanced view of Islaam, explaining and clarifying not only beliefs but also discussing actions, both beneficial and harmful, both permissible and forbidden, all of which are related to the issue of purifying ourselves inwardly and outwardly. Sheikh al-Ismaa'eelee in his work *'Itiqaad Ahlus-Sunnah* stated,[13]

> *"They (the people of the Sunnah) hold that what is required is turning and staying away from innovation in the religion, from general transgression and wrongdoing, arrogance, and conceitedness. They hold that what is required is refraining from that which causes harm or injury to others and leaving impermissible backbiting except towards the one who openly practices some form of innovation or the following of personal whims and*

[13] 'Itiqaad Ahlus-Sunnah pg. 53

desires, calling to both of these. Such that warning and clarifying speech about such people is not considered impermissible backbiting in the view of their scholars."

Likewise Sheikh al-Islaam Abu Ismaa'eel as-Saaboonee, who came in the next century after Sheikh al-Ismaa'eelee, stated in his work *'Aqeedah as-Salaf Ahlul-Hadeeth*, [14]

"They hold that the Muslims should be prompt in the performance of the obligatory prayers, and they recommend and encourage the standing at night in non-obligatory prayer after sleeping a portion of the night, and the requirement of maintaining good family relations in all respects, and the spreading of the greeting of salaam among the Muslims, and the feeding of food to those categories of people for whom this is encouraged in the Sunnah...and encouraging without any delay the doing and undertaking of every type of good and beneficial action, as well as the distancing and staying away of the people who stand upon innovation in the religion and various forms of misguidance..."

Likewise Sheikh Ismaa'eel al-Asfahaanee, who came in the next century after Sheikh as-Saaboonee, stated in his work *al-Hujjah fee Bayan al-Muhujjah*, [15]

"It is from the way and methodology of Ahlus-Sunnah to have fear and caution in what they consume of food and drink, and to stay away from all form of sexual sins and shameful offensive actions, to stay away and distance themselves from the misguided people whose way is following their desires and to abandon them, to encourage and without delay undertake doing every type of good and beneficial action, and to hold back from entering and getting involved with misconceptions and doubtful matters..."

---

[14] 'Aqeedah as-Salah Ahlul-Hadeeth pg. 92
[15] al-Hujjah fee Bayan al-Muhujjah: vol. 2, pg. 52

23

Likewise Sheikh al-Islaam Ibn Taymeeyah, who lived some centuries after Sheikh Ismaa'eel al-Asfahaanee, and who some wrongly believe initially turned Muslims towards looking back to the Companions and the first generations of Muslims, also described this comprehensive understanding of what is Islaam, which was reflected by the previous steadfast scholars. [16]

> *"They enjoin upon the people to be patient when facing trials and difficulties, and to have thankfulness to Allaah when ease and comfort reach them. They call and invite to having the noblest of character and to the engaging in the best of good deeds and endeavors.*
>
> *They believe fully in the meaning of the statement of the Prophet, may the praise and salutations of Allaah be upon him, {**The believers who show the most perfect Faith are those who have the best behavior...**} Such that they generally recommend that the people keep relations with those who cut ties with them, generally spend upon those who do not spend upon them, and excuse the one who does you some injustice.*
>
> *They enjoin excellent treatment of one's parents, maintaining family ties and relations, treating one's neighbors well, treating well the orphans, the poor, and travelers, and to deal gently with those over whom you have authority.*
>
> *They forbid acting with arrogance, vanity, and tyranny over others, as well as being overbearing and dominating over the people of creation, whether with some justification and right or without it.*
>
> *They are those who enjoin upon the people to have the best of character as Muslims and warn and prevent them*

---

[16] As narrated in the commentary of Sheikh Muhammad Khalil Harras of Aqeedatul-Waasiteeyah, pg. 258-259

> *from having inferior and bad character. Everything which they state and act upon in this area, and all other areas, is done upon their being of those who follow and adhere to the Book of Allaah and the Sunnah, with their way and methodology being the religion of Islaam which Allaah revealed and sent down to Muhammad, may the praise and salutations of Allaah be upon him."*

Lastly, his well known student upon the way of the Salaf, Ibn al-Qayyim, expressing the undeniable connection between character and behavior and the entire religion of Islaam, stated, [17]

> *"Chapter: The religion of Islaam is all good character and behavior, whenever you are increased in having excellent character, you are increased in the excellence of your religion."*

And he mentioned within this same section of this work,

> *"...Good character is built upon four pillars, without which it is not conceivable to build it: having patience, excusing of others, courage, and acting with justice...*
>
> *And poor and bad character stems and grows out of four pillars: ignorance, acting unjustly, the following of desires, and getting angry."*

This clarifies what the Salaf, and Salafee scholars have always called to, by Allaah's mercy. Their writing and works all reflect that it is not possible to separate the only correct way of purifying the soul from the correct beliefs and methodology of the people of the Sunnah through the centuries.

This is also something which is true for the modern day leading scholars who truly live and defend the Sunnah, just as it was in previous centuries. Indeed, we have been blessed with many small works just collecting the accounts of excellent character and behavior in every area

[17]   Madaarij as-Saalikeen: vol.2 pg. 307

of good character witnessed by the general people of our age from the noble leading scholars of this age like Sheikh Ibn Baaz, Sheikh al-'Utheimeen, and Sheikh al-Albaanee, may Allaah have abundant mercy upon them all.

Yet something important that distinguishes their way from the many diverse ever-changing paths of the Sufee orders and organizations is that these guided scholars, and the Muslims who benefit from their knowledge, have satisfied themselves with the clear Sunnah, not innovations, as the means to purify one's souls and gain entry into Jannah. They have always focused on firstly correcting fundamental beliefs and the true foundation for success, and upon establishing the unchanging practices and acts of legitimate worship which the Messenger taught us, not new forms that later generations developed. This satisfaction which Sufees consider restrictive, by not turning to those new matters some consider "good innovations", we consider as being satisfied with the true religion which Allaah sent down complete and perfect, and keeping our faces turned clearly toward the beautiful Sunnah, which satisfies our thirst for guidance.

The scholars upon the way of the Salaf strongly emphasize and give priority to first establishing the correct beliefs in the hearts of the Muslims, because this is the only correct methodology of building the foundation of emaan, just as every prophet and messenger did. This way recognizes that our outward actions and deeds are only a true reflection of, and firmly built upon, those inward aspects of emaan and authentic beliefs. Such that when we hear our scholars like as Sheikh al-'Utheimeen, may Allaah have mercy upon him, discuss the outward reality of the Muslims today saying,[18]

> *"The person who carefully examines what the people stand upon in their lives in many of the Muslim lands, clearly finds the strangeness of the true religion of Islaam*

[18] al-Qawl al-Mufeed: vol. 1 pg. 306

and the turning away of the people from implementing Allaah's right to be worshiped alone."

We must know that this is caused, in part, by the inward deficiencies we have as Muslims. For this reason, Sheikh al-Islaam Ibn Taymeeyah, said, [19]

"If there is a deficiency in an obligatory outward action, then this is due to a deficiency within one's emaan or faith within the heart. Since it is not conceivable that someone with the obligatory complete faith inwardly in the heart would fail to also reflect that in the proper performance of outward obligatory deeds.

Imaam ash-Shaatibee, a distinguished scholar with several works discussing the important fundamental and foundational principles of the religion of Islaam, said,[20]

"Outward actions in the Sharee'ah are an indication of what is found within someone inwardly. Such that if their outward behavior is damaged and deficient or it is steadfast and upright, then the judgement is that the inward state is similar to it."

Yet these scholars, in the same works that reflect the importance that they gave to character and behavior, also gave tremendous importance to distinguishing innovations, warning against any new matters brought into Islaam, and distinguishing them from the authentic transmitted practices of the Messenger of Allaah. Imaam ash-Shaatibee narrated in the remarkable work, entitled al-'Istisaam,

"Abu 'Alee al-Hasan Ibn 'Alee al-Jawzajaanee said, "From the signs or indicators of a worshiper of Allaah being blessed with contentment and success are:

the obedience of Allaah being made easy for him,

---

[19] Majmu'a al-Fataawa vol.7 pg. 582
[20] al-Muwaafiqaat, vol 1 pg. 233

that his actions and endeavors conform and agree with the Sunnah,

that his companions and associates are the people of goodness and rectification,

that he has excellent character in dealing with his Muslim brothers.

that he is generous in bringing good and goodness to the creation

that he has significant concern for the well-being of the Muslims

and that he respects and takes care of his time.

He was also asked about the ways to come closer to Allaah? He replied,

*"The ways of coming closer to Allaah are numerous. The clearest of ways and those furthest away from what is doubtful is: through following the Sunnah in statements, deeds, purpose and determination, beliefs, and intention. As Allaah has said, ❨**If you obey him, you shall be on the right guidance...**❩-(Surah an-Nur: 54)*

So it was said to him, "What is the way towards the Sunnah?"

He replied, "It is by staying far away from innovations in the religion, by uniting upon that which the scholars of Islaam of the first generation stood together upon as the truth, while staying far away from the gatherings of philosophical discussion and the people connected to them. It is by holding firmly to the path of following established guidance.

*This is what has been commanded for us by the Prophet, may Allaah's praise and salutations be upon him, through the statement of Allaah, ❋**Then, We have inspired you (O Muhammad saying): "Follow the religion of Ibraaheem (Abraham) Hanifa (Islaamic Monotheism - to worship none but Allaah)**❋-(Surah an-Nahl: 123)"*

A related common misconception, found among many people affected by the misguiding speech of the modern callers to traditional Sufism is found in the statement, ***"But aren't there many ways to come closer to Allaah?"*** Ibn Taymeeyah, may Allaah have mercy upon him, who wrote extensively in evidenced examinations and discussions about the misguidance found among the Sufees and philosophers in his age, was asked about this saying of claiming that the paths to Allaah are numerous. He replied,[21]

"...If what is intended by this expression are those many actions which are affirmed in the Sharee'ah and which conform to the source texts of the Qur'aan and Sunnah, like performing ritual prayers, giving charity, striving in Allaah's path, the various form of dhikr, and reading and reciting, then this is a true statement.

But if what is intended by it is seeking closeness to Allaah through some way or methodology which opposes and contradicts aspects of the guidance of the Book of Allaah and the Sunnah, then this is a statement of falsehood."

He, may Allaah have mercy upon him, clarified that there is an essential difference between the correct understanding that there are multiple possible permissible actions leading a Muslim towards coming closer to Allaah, meaning valid ways of pleasing Allaah that specifically conform to the revealed guidance of Islaam, and the false understanding

---

[21] Mamu'a al-Fataawaa vol. 10 pg. 260

that there are multiple paths and methodologies which can all be considered valid ways of gaining closeness to, and pleasing, Allaah. By this, meaning newly adopted, practices not known to the first Muslims or our beloved Messenger. There is no doubt that every sincere Muslim should affirm that the issues of purifying one's soul and rectification are directly related to having the correct beliefs of Islaam, as the Prophet taught us. Every sincere Muslim should affirm that focusing upon purification of the soul first needs laying the proper basic foundation of correct understanding and beliefs for your overall rectification as a worshiper of Allaah. It is for this reason that Ibn Taymeeyah also mentioned,[22]

> *"The issues of upright behavior or poor behavior are considered an aspect of the overall realm of the general issues of beliefs. All of them are based upon the guidance of the source texts found within the Book of Allaah and the Sunnah."*

Discussing the false idea that as time passes, Islaam should accept any new and varied way of seeking self purification and rectification which people adopt, regardless of whether it has or lacks a clear basis in the authentic Sunnah, Ibn al-Qayyim said,[23]

> *"The one who directs you towards something as part of the religion which is not based upon 'he informed us' and 'he narrated to us,' is directing you towards a matter which is either from the misguided delusion of some of the Sufees, or a invalid analogy based upon the way of philosophical speculations, or limited personal opinions.*
>
> *Since after the guidance of the Qur'aan and what is received by means of that knowledge transmitted through the means of "he informed us" and "he narrated to us," there are only the misconceptions of the people engaged*

[22] Majmu'a al-Fataawa: vol.19 pg. 273
[23] Madaarij as-Saalikeen vol.2 pg. 468

30

in harmful philosophical rhetoric, or the false views of those who have deviated away from revealed guidance, or the delusions conceived by the Sufees, or the baseless analogies of the philosophers.

Anyone who separates himself from the established sources of evidence goes far far astray. Whereas there is nothing which truly guides towards Allaah, and Jannah, other than the Book of Allaah and the Sunnah. "

In fact, just as is affirmed in all the works of the scholars upon the way of the first believing generations, Ibn al-Qayyim makes clear that Islaam already affirmed the many valid ways to accomplish good and seek Allaah's pleasure, without needing the also adopt what some wrongly consider "good innovations" brought into Islaam for its alleged betterment,[24]

"From among the people are those whose main endeavor, which they undertake and is the primary path and focus which they spend their time seeking Allaah's pleasure upon, is connected to knowledge and teaching until they reach success in it through Allaah's leave.

And from among the people are those whose main endeavor which they undertake is engaging in accepted statements of remembrance, making them what they seek increase with Allaah upon, what they continually engages in, and their most precious activity.

And from among the people are those whose main endeavor and focus is the ritual prayers.

And from among them is the one who makes his primary path and focus the doing of good and benefiting people generally, such as assisting them with their needs, alleviating suffering and distress, and various types of

---

[24] Tareeq al-Hijratayn: pg.178

giving charity to others.

And from them are those who spend their time seeking Allaah's pleasure in every possible way available and open to them, and with every type of good they have a role and share. Wherever there is any valid form or expression of uboodeyyah or submissive worship of Allaah, you will find them involved in it some way.

Such that if it is related to beneficial knowledge you find him with those Muslim engaged in that.

Or it if is related to striving in Jihaad, you find him within the ranks of those undertaking that Jihad upon the guidelines of the Sharee'ah, or if it is related to performing the ritual prayer, he is with those standing forth in its performance.

Or if it is related to the performance of accepted statements of remembrance, he is of those engaged in this.

Or if it is an endeavor of generally doing good and bringing benefit to people, you find him among that group of those workers of good striving in that. And if you were to ask him what do you intend through your actions and endeavors, he would reply 'I only intend to fulfill the commandments of my Lord wherever I am able.'

So we absolutely reject the false belief that there is any good a worshiper can do that is not founded in the revealed guidance of the Qur'aan and Sunnah as understood and practiced by the Messenger of Allaah, his Companions, and those who followed them step by step in goodness throughout the centuries.

Additionally, after looking closely at the guidance of the Messenger of Allaah, we say that from those secondary righteous examples we should consider is not some well know Sufee sheikh who has delved deeply into the inward "heights and realms" of mysticism, one who claims to allegedly have gained a high level of closeness to Allaah. But it is someone whose incredible life can teach you by reflecting what he learned directly from the best of creation - our beloved Messenger of Allaah, may the praise and salutations of Allaah be upon him - since he grew in Islaam at his hand. It is the best of all humanity after the prophets and messengers - Abu Bakr, may Allaah be pleased with him. This is shown clearly in many authentic narrations, such as the following, [25]

{Abu Hurairah reported that Allaah's Messenger said to us: Who amongst you is fasting today?

Abu Bakr said: I am. He then said: Who amongst you followed a funeral procession today?

Abu Bakr said: I did. He (the Prophet) then said: Who amongst you served food to the needy?

Abu Bakr said: I did. He (again) said: Who amongst you has today visited the sick?

Abu Bakr said: I did. Thereupon Allaah's Messenger said:

Anyone in whom these good deeds are combined will certainly enter Paradise.}

The way of the Salaf understood seeking closeness to Allaah is shown beautifully in this hadeeth about Abu Bakr, may Allaah be pleased with him.

Consider carefully my Muslim brother or sister, that the way of Abu Bakr is firmly grounded and steeped, at every step and turn, upon the revealed religion taught to him by his beloved Messenger, without any innovation at all. Likewise, there is no doubt that the result of the

[25] Saheeh Muslim 1028

way of following guidance proceeded upon by Abu Bakr, led to him being given glad tidings of entering Paradise. When one reads some of the various commentaries of the scholars of the Sunnah about some of the beneficial inward effects of these legislated actions mentioned in the above narration, we understand how, what is found in the Sunnah, truly affects and enriches the inner state of any Muslim who properly engages in them. So let us consider the true effect of his following, and being satisfied, with the Sunnah.

In this narration he engaged in the practice of fasting which builds and develops taqwa, or the fear of Allaah, inwardly and outwardly, when done according to the Sunnah. In this narration is included remembering death and remembering to focus on the Hereafter, by following the funeral procession when done according to the Sunnah. In this narration he engaged in visiting the sick and feeding the poor Muslims, which helps develop thankfulness and gratitude to Allaah in the heart, when done according to the Sunnah. All of these are aspects of self purification and cultivating the believer's heart, which naturally are produced through truly following the Sunnah.

If it is said: but not all of the Sufees neglect these matters! Indeed that is true, but all of them who adopt any new practice, belief, or methodology, have neglected or turned away from the fundamental truth in Islaam that the true guidance of every Muslim lies in making the revealed guidance the sole criterion and model to follow. They have turned away from truly being satisfied with just that. This is what the best generation of humanity did -the Companions of the Messengers of Allaah, may Allaah be pleased with all of them. This is what Abu Bakr, may Allaah be pleased with him, did, may Allaah be pleased with him, and increase the love we have of all of the noble Companions.

May Allaah protect us from turning away from the best example after the Prophet, Abu Bakr, may Allaah be pleased with him, who was fully satisfied with the simple clear religion. That satisfaction led to his rectification and purification as a worshiper of Allaah, without adding and calling to a single new belief, a single new specific statement of dhikr, or single new form of worship, such as supplicating through the righteous dead Muslims in their graves. None of these devised practices common among today's Sufees can be found in the life of Abu Bakr, may Allaah be pleased with him, except those which are already found in the authentic Sunnah! Certainly he truly exemplified and implemented the guidance of the Qur'aan where Allaah has said, *Say (O Muhammad to mankind): If you really love Allaah, then follow me, Allaah will love you and forgive you your sins. And Allaah is Oft-Forgiving, Most Merciful.*-(Surah Aal-'Imraan: 31).

So we say, as our scholars say, that the general guidelines for the ways of doing good, gaining closeness to Allaah, and reaching paradise are evidenced, known, and long since established by the believer's way of the Companions, and whatever goes beyond their path in adherence to the Sunnah is falsehood and futile. Considering where one's chosen way of purification of the souls comes from is something essential for any sincere Muslim who truly seeks self-purification, due to the many pleasing claims and enticing subtle calls present today.

The one who carefully looks into the guidance of the Qur'aan, with a sincere and accepting heart, finds that true purification of the souls is fundamentally tied directly to the tawheed that the first Muslims made their foundation. They find that it is essentially connected to the true worship of Allaah alone and separating ourselves from its opposite, Shirk, meaning the sin and transgression of associating others in that worship due to Allaah alone.

They find that proceeding upon a path or program of successful purification is only established and realized through following revelation not through innovation.

Likewise, it is also found in the statements of the clarifying scholars, the important point that Allaah directly connects true purification to outward good deeds, such as those mentioned in the hadeeth about Abu Bakr, not only the inward state of the heart. This is clearly affirmed in many verses of the Qur'aan. Allaah, the Most High, says, ◈ *But whoever comes to Him as a believer, and has done righteous good deeds, for such are the high ranks, `Adn Gardens, under which rivers flow, wherein they will abide forever, and such is the reward of those who purify themselves.*◈-(Surah Ta-Ha:75-76) and many other similar verses. The noble scholar Ibn Katheer, whose explanation of the Qur'aan was based upon the interpretations of the early Muslims, explained the meaning of this verse as first and foremost related to the issues of worshiping Allaah alone and the destructive highest sin of associating others with Him in worship, and related to following the fundamental guidance the prophets and messengers came with. This is found in his words:[26]

"....(*and such is the reward of those who purify themselves.*) *meaning one who purifies himself from dirt, filth and associating partners with Allaah. This is the person who worships Allaah alone, without ascribing partners to Him, and he follows the Messengers in the good they came with and all that they claim.*"

[26] Tafseer Ibn Katheer: vol. 3 pg. 156

We find that there are many different types of misguidance and innovations witnessed in the area of purification of the self or soul. Some people believe that these new innovated practices, or revived old innovated practices of organized collective dhikr, are only small matters that help us better learn to worship Allaah. In this way they further the false claim about the place of so-called "good innovations" in Islaam. Yet the reality is, as Sheikh al-'Utheimeen, may Allaah have mercy upon him, clarified, [27]

> *"There is no doubt regarding innovation in the religion that some forms of innovation are lesser than others. Yet what is upon a person to do is to be warned from innovation generally, and be one who closely follows the methodology of Islaam proceeded upon by the first generations of Islaam."*

The sincere Muslim should also ask himself firstly about that "Sheikh" who decided that adding to the religion was needed, and so took it upon himself to further "improve" Islaam and develop these so called minor adapted forms and practices of dhikr to help purify our souls. How can he believe he has the right and authority to develop and add to those many affirmed acts of worship within the pure religion which truly develop and cultivate us as Muslims? Furthermore, for the one practicing these new ways,, why would a Muslim think that the practices within the Sunnah that were taught to the Noble Companions are not sufficient for him? Sheikh Ahmad ibn Yahya An-Najmee, may Allaah have mercy upon him, discusses this saying,[28]

---

[27]   al-Qawl al-Mufeed: vol. 1 pg. 424
[28]   Fath Rabb al-Bareeyat Alaa Kitaab Aham al-Muhimaat: pg 97

"The person upon innovation is someone claiming to be a partner or contributor in putting forth what is to be considered as the Sharee'ah just as if he was saying, "I have knowledge of a beneficial matter or practice which Allaah did not teach the Messenger of Allaah." Therefore, Maalik Ibn Anas, may Allaah have mercy upon him, said, 'The one who knowingly follows some innovation, is someone indirectly accusing the Prophet Muhammad with treachery in not delivering all of the message of Islaam.'

As such, it is obligatory to warn against all forms and types of innovation -that which is seen as minor as well as that which is clearly significant, that which is related to devised beliefs and that which is related to innovated actions. One should live upon the Sunnah, as this is the best thing a person can seek to do within his life in order to protect himself from facing punishment after his death.

Note: It is required that we know that innovation should be understood to be what is newly introduced in the religion of Islaam, as something under the banner of Islaam and attributed to Islaam. As for those scientific matters of development in worldly endeavors and newly developed technologies related to this, then this does not fall into this correct definition of innovation in Islaam, and is not considered from it. And the success is from Allaah alone."

Here it is important to mention a dangerous misconception related to the field of efforts to teach and call to Islaam. This is the fact that some callers who, despite holding some of the core beliefs of the people of the Sunnah, wrongly hold that we should not discuss and clarify our differences with those who call to the new innovated practices found with the many different tareeqahs or paths and orders of

Sufism.

Some go even further, saying that we should remain silent about some affirmed aspects that we know without question to be part of the authentic beliefs of Islaam based upon the Qur'aan and Sunnah, so as to not show disagreement with those Muslims who are Sufees. Yet Sheikh al-'Utheimeen, may Allaah have mercy upon him, clarified the significant error of this false perspective and aspect of one's methodology, when answering the following question, [29]

Question: Some of our brothers in this country who are callers to Allaah, the Most Glorified and the Most Exalted, view that it is for an overall benefit that they stand in agreement with the Sufees upon not speaking during their lectures or sermons about matters such as affirming Allaah's ascendency of the Throne in a manner suiting His Majesty, or the clear Sharee'ah ruling about not calling upon and supplicating for assistance and help from other than Allaah when in need, as well as other distinguishing issues.

They derive and support their position from the fact that the Prophet, may Allaah's praise and salutations be upon him, made a peace treaty with the Jewish tribes of Medina. Is this derivation and conclusion correct sheikh? What is your guidance regarding it?

*Answer: "This conclusion they have reached is not sound, and isn't correct. Because in fact this is actually what Allaah the Most High has mentioned in the verse ﴿**They wish that you should compromise (in religion out of courtesy) with them, so they (too) would compromise with you.**﴾- (Surah al-Qalam: 9) Compromise within the religion is not permissible.*

---

[29] Open Door Gatherings: cassette 156

The Messenger, upon him be Allaah's praise and salutations, established his treaty with the Jewish tribes upon the agreement that neither party would commit any acts of aggression against the other, not that the Muslims would be pleased and affirm their religious practices -never! It is not possible that the Messenger of Allaah ever be pleased with their religious practices -ever. And that which you mentioned includes being pleased with what those Sufees stand upon of falsehood. This action, which they present as something of overall benefit, is in reality, actually an impermissible compromise. Such compromise is forbidden in Islaam.

It is not permissible for anyone to compromise with another regarding that which is in the religion of Allaah. Rather it is an obligation to clarify and make the truth of a matter apparent to everyone. However, it is possible to correctly view that it may not be for the overall or general benefit to start by criticizing those various matters which are incorrect before speaking about anything else, and that one should start with correctly explaining what is sound and correct.

For example, if you speak about the issues of Allaah's transcendence, as you mentioned, then you explain the correct meaning of His rising (in a manner befitting His majesty), and clarify its reality without first bringing forth that there are such and such people who incorrectly interpret this to mean such and such. Only doing this after the people have become accustomed to the issue and come to properly understand the truth of it. This is in order to make it easy for them moving from what is falsehood to what is the truth."

Similarly, Sheikh Ahmad Ibn Yahya An-Najmee, may Allaah have mercy upon him, said about the confusion caused by many people claiming to be from the people of the Sunnah,[30]

"There have come forward various different people in the present age who claim that they are from the people of the Sunnah. While at the same time they take as a basis for their rulings, and as part of the Sharee'ah, different statements from their leading people who are not infallible, as only the Prophet was.

Such as the statement from one of their leaders who said, [We cooperate with each other in those issue in which we agree, and we simply excuse each other in those matters we disagree upon.]. How could we possibly excuse each other about everything we disagree upon?

*Does Allaah excuse the one who brings into Islaam some newly developed matter of innovation -that neither Allaah not His Messenger came with? No, by Allaah such a person is not excused for this. Rather as the hadeeth states, {**The one who brings forth a new matter in this religion of ours -that is not part of it, that matter is rejected**.}*

Some of these people say to those who follow them, [We will fast all together collectively, either in the second or fifth day of the week, or during the days of the full moon, and then we will also break our fasts collectively all together.]

Ok, then our question is: Did the Prophet, may the praise and salutations of Allaah be upon him, ever say to his own Companions, 'We will fast all together collectively...' No, he never did. Not a single Companion

---

[30] Audio selection in the voice of the Sheikh from a lecture entitled "Unfurled Banners of the Sunnah." cassettes numbered 197 & 198

reported that he ever even once said that.

The same situation of innovation is the case with the call to make the pledge of allegiance to this person or that leader, or the call focusing on establishing the governmental system of the khalifah, and the many various claims similar to these. These are all matters that clearly have no basis within the authentic Sunnah. Yet despite that, the people openly calling to them all claim that they are from the people of the Sunnah!

No, by Allaah, they are not from the people of the Sunnah, rather the true Sunnah and its people of free from them and what they claim. For this reason, every individual who innovates something new into Islaam, then certainly the Sunnah is distinguished and distinct from their religious innovation.

Those who say that it is acceptable and permissible to revolt and overthrow the Muslim governmental leaders are people who have wrongly taken from the way and methodology of the misguided sect of the Khawaarij.

Those who declare some of the sinning Muslims as disbelievers due to the major sins they commit are likewise taking this from the way and methodology of the Khawaarij, as well as from the sect of the Mu'tazilah. And there are many different examples of this from different innovated claims.

Therefore it is an obligation upon a Muslim who desires to be successful to clearly learn what are the actual practices of the Sunnah, so that he is saved from falling into these new innovations as if they were the Sunnah.

But as for the one who remains ignorant, in a state where he does not have the knowledge to distinguish, then these people will continue to be able to conceal their innovation and mislead him, by falsely saying "We stand upon the Sunnah and are not opposing anything from the Sunnah...."

Every Muslim should know that there is significant danger in taking on and adopting any newly developed path or program of self rectification or general worship which was unknown to the Companions of the Prophet, may Allaah be pleased with them all. As certainly among the Companions were the first and the most knowledgeable scholars of Islaam, after it's Messenger. As Sheikh Ahmad an-Najmee, may Allaah have mercy upon him, mentioned in another work, [31]

"...The reference in distinguishing between newly invented matters in the religion and those affirmed matters which have a Sharee'ah basis and support are those scholars who have worked with the Sharee'ah and its knowledge for a long amount of time, and who generally are found to be in a condition of steadfastness upon uprightness and guidance."

---

[31] Ta'sees al-Ahkaam Sharh Amdat al-'Ahkaam vol. 5: 139

A key element of true self rectification is a continuous earnest self-accounting as found in the Sunnah and in the practices of the early Muslims. Ibn al-Qayyim, may Allaah have mercy upon him, explained this clearly stating, [32]

> *"The purification of the self or soul and its becoming rectified is dependent upon it being called to account and assessed. There is no purification or rectification, nor any possibility of it being brought to a state of well-being, except through calling oneself to account. al-Hasan al-Basree, may Allaah have mercy upon him, said, 'As for the believer, then you do not see him in any other state except as one who steps forth and confronts himself saying:*
>
> *Why did I make such and such statement? Why did I eat such and such food? Why did I go to such and such place? Why did I do this thing? Why did I engage in that matter? By Allaah, I will not fall into that again" and what is similar to theses statements. He takes himself to account looking at his shortcomings and deficiencies so that he has the opportunity to try to fix and rectify them.' "*

He, may Allaah have mercy upon him, also spoke about the state of the one who does not practice this and what that results in, saying, [33]

> *"It is not for the one who is an adult and someone responsible to fall into heedlessness, turning away from self examination and calling himself to account, simply letting oneself act in any manner, and being lax in important matters and simply going where they might be led. Acting this way only leads to your own ruin.*

[32] Madaarij as-Saalikeen: vol. 2 pg. 510
[33] Ighaathatul-Lahfaan: vol. 1 pg. 136

Moreover, this is the way of the people who are arrogant -they shut their eyes to their faults and wrongs, expect and count on eventually being excused and forgiven. Therefore they neglect calling themselves to account and looking at their own faults and shortcomings. Additionally, if such a person actually turns to examine himself, often he is still not bothered by his sins, as he has become accustomed to and numbingly comfortable with them, such that weaning and pulling himself away from them is something quite difficult."

One of the early righteous individuals, Maymoon Ibn Mahraan, said,[34]

"A man will not be considered from among the people who correctly fears Allaah until he is someone who personally calls himself to account with more diligence than we examine and investigate our business affairs and financial pursuits, until he knows well from what efforts or wealth his food comes from, from what efforts or wealth his clothing comes from, from what efforts or wealth his drink comes from- whether from that which is permissible or what has been made forbidden."

On this important subject, Ibn Taymeeyah, mentioned, [35]

"A person and their deeds will not become purified until it has removed what opposes and conflicts with that desired purity. Such that a man cannot become someone successful in self-purification until he turns away from and abandons evil and wrongdoing. As that wrongdoing tarnishes and pollutes an individual and works its way into him. Ibn Qutaybah said, 'It pollutes him, meaning weakens him through the immorality and wrongdoing he is committing.' "

---

[34]   Hilyaatyl-Awleeyah vol. 4 number 89
[35]   Majmu'a al-Fataawa vol. 10 pg. 629

There are many things of different levels of importance that people engage in that may prevent them from giving suitable focus to self purification as found within the Sunnah. One, which affects many people today, is a constant preoccupation with following the news and reading news articles. Alhamdulillah the scholars have explained that there is a way to not be over occupied and take what is beneficial while leaving what is harmful in modern news and media. The guiding scholar Sheikh Ibn Baaz, may Allaah have mercy upon him, was asked, *"It is well know that the majority of what is produced and put out on the different forms of media such as television, and similar means, that the vast majority of it contains bad behavior, shameless comedy and joking, what is entirely immoral and wicked, despite there being rare exceptions to this. As such, in this situation, should we implement the Sharee'ah principle of giving precedence to preventing evil over gaining some benefit in relation to the media? May Allaah grant you steadfastness."* He replied,[36]

> *Answer: This Sharee'ah guideline is a tremendous principle in Islaam which should always be applied to our affairs. This being that the essential importance of preventing possible evil and harmful outcomes, coming from a matter, must take precedence over achieving some possible beneficial results and outcomes which may be produced through it. Because preventing harm should always be given more importance than gaining a possible benefit or form of good.*
>
> *In regard to these different forms of media, what is obligatory is that the ruling Muslim authorities are advised about their management by the scholars and prominent individuals, and that the common Muslims offer advice between themselves as to the best ways to use*

[36] Ruling number 1724 from the Sheikh's website

them beneficially. They all must warn against what is harmful within them, whether that occurs in the media of this land, or in that coming from other countries and places. It is an obligation to warn against any evil and wrongdoing they have, and not simply indulge or engage in it.

Similarly, we should be pleased with the truth that some programs promote, and listen to and take from them. They same applies to what is found in newspapers, we must take whatever good they have while leaving and turning away from that offensive and disagreeable material they contain. A believer must be very selective in what they take, and not simply take from anyone and everyone, and accept from anywhere and everywhere. This also applies to audio media channels and to print media which is read, meaning take from it that which Islaam considers good and beneficial and push away what they contain of evil and harmful material.

Alhamdulillah, in this land the people of knowledge continually advise and guide the rulers and authorities in this area. We ask Allaah to benefit us through understanding and practicing the reasons for being successful and guided, and that He grant the Muslim authorities success in being guided to every matter which contains that which rectifies both the Muslim lands and Muslim worshipers. Indeed, He is the best of those to be in charge of our affairs."

Yet this is not what we often see from many Muslims, who spend significant amount of time reading, discussing, debating, and commenting, with little discretion or selection, on whatever is currently found in the news. It is for this reasons that scholar Sheikh al-Fauzaan, may Allaah preserve him, warns us that,[37]

---

[37] Beneficial Answers the Question Regarding Modern Methodologies: pg. 103

> *"...Occupying oneself with general news programs and news reports regarding the various events that happen within the world without having clear knowledge of the beliefs of Islaam, and without having knowledge generally of the matters of the Sharee'ah causes misguidance and personal loss. It leads the one who spends his time this way to be someone whose thoughts are confused and chaotic, because he has substituted that which is inferior for that which is better and guiding."*

At the very minimum, it often becomes something which prevents and acts as a barrier to what would truly assist them in their lives of beneficial knowledge. Sheikh Ahmad Ibn Yahya An-Najmee, may Allaah have mercy upon him, said,[38]

> *"Today, one can see many of the people who regularly and consistently read certain published magazines, purchasing them everyday and reading whatever news reports they contain. Yet perhaps a month goes by, and they have not even opened the Book of Allaah not to recite it generally, nor to read it and carefully consider its guidance. For such an individual, he should fear that misguidance would eventually overtake him. Because this can be considered wrongfully neglecting the Book of Allaah, and focusing upon which does not actually benefit, or which only benefits you to a very small degree. And certainly from Allaah we came and to Him we will return.*
>
> *By Allaah, you would be shocked, as if you were to give to someone of this description a book to read by which he can actually benefit in his general understanding and his beliefs of Islam, or by which he can benefit in some other way which would strengthen his faith, that perhaps he may take it from you but later just throw to*

---

[38] Fath ar-Raheem al-Wadood fe at-Taa'leeq alaa Kitaab as-Sunnah min Sunan al-Imaam Abee Dawud

the side not even really looking at it. And perhaps such a person would not even take or accept the book you were offering him in the first place!

So certainly, I call and invite such individuals to turn and give attention to the Book of Allaah, and to give attention to the Sunnah of the Messenger of Allaah. They should give importance and focus on that which will benefit them with Allaah the Most Perfect and the Most High, that which is better for them than the news of current world events which do not benefit a worshiper of Allaah anything in the Hereafter. It is mainly only a distraction which engages your attention for short while. And certainly from Allaah we came and to Him we will return. And the success is from Allaah"

Sheikh al-Albaanee, may Allaah have mercy upon him, also made an important distinction,[39]

"I believe that that which assists a Muslim scholar to have the capacity to address and help rectify the different events and issues which occur, and which he is asked about by the people, is that he becomes someone who knows the relevant news and those current events which happen. And there is no means for him to do so except through reading and listening to the media, whether this is by means of the radio or by reading newspapers and magazines.

I say this, despite bearing witness that I am from those who are the furthest from putting this into practice at present, as that which I undertake of working to serve the sciences of the Sunnah is enough for me.

But I do not blame the one who directs his attention to study these media, and to these sources, with the clear condition that they be someone who is knowledgeable of

---

[39] Silsilaat al-Hudaa wa an-Nur audio tape series no. 704

Islaam, and not be a general Muslim who possesses very little knowledge..."

Sheikh al-Albaanee, may Allaah have mercy upon him, also explained the general methodology of the first Muslims in relation to this issue[40]

"...As for engaging at length in obtaining news, knowledge of armed conflicts and western politics, then this is generally from the aspect of: "Knowledge of something is better than being ignorant of it." So this is something that we do not forsake. However, at the same time, we must not be very enthusiastic and fanatical about it.

This is since the Prophet, may the praise and salutations of Allaah be upon him, did not establish the affair of his Companions on knowing and following precisely, the news of his enemies to the same extent as he, may the praise and salutations of Allaah be upon him, used to focus on teaching his Companions knowledge from one perspective and cultivating them on fulfilling Allaah's commands from another perspective."

Yet how many people neglect the reading of the preserved Qur'aan or neglect cultivating our families upon beneficial knowledge from the unchanging guidance of Islaam, but diligently keep up with the current news and events which will only change tomorrow?! So look, my brother or sister, to where you put that valuable time you will be asked about on the Day of Judgement.

Another related pitfall that prevents some from working upon their own rectification, is an unbalanced focus upon other people causing them to neglect focusing upon themselves. Sheikh Saaleh Fauzaan al-Fauzaan, may Allaah preserve him, was asked, [41]

[40] The Fataawaa of Shaikh al-Albaanee from al-Asaalah Magazine, p. 22 found in Al-Asaalah Magazine, Issue #18 originally translated by Ismaa'eel Alarcon
[41] A Selection of Islamic Rulings: Ruling no 1663

Is it permissible for a person to individually place himself as one who judges other people in every situation or stance? When is it permissible according to the guidelines of the Sharee'ah for a person to state about another: "This person is someone wicked," and "This other person is not like that."? He replied,

"It isn't proper for a person to individually place himself as one who judges other people and forgets or neglects himself and his own condition. Rather, what a person should do is look towards recognizing the errors they have themselves firstly, before they look towards the errors of others.

Yet, if a Muslim places himself as someone who offers advice to his brothers enjoining what is good and forbidding what is wrongdoing, then this is a good matter of benefit. But not someone simply placing himself as one who judges other people. Allaah, the Most High, says, ❊**The believers are nothing else than brothers (in Islamic religion). So make reconciliation between your brothers, and fear Allaah, that you may receive mercy.**❊-(Surah al-Hujuraat: 10) And the Messenger, may Allaah's praise and salutations be upon him, said, {**A believer is like a brick for another believer, the one supporting the other.**} (Saheeh Muslim: 2585) And Allaah, the Most High, says, ❊**Help you one another in al-birr and at-taqwa (virtue, righteousness and piety); but do not help one another in sin and transgression.**❊-(Surah al-Ma'idah: 2) And the Messenger, may Allaah's praise and salutations be upon him, said, {**"The religion is giving advice and well wishing." So we said, "For whom, Messenger of Allaah?" He said, "For Allaah, His Book, His Messenger and for the leaders and the general Muslims."**} (Saheeh Muslim from the narration of Tameem ad-Daaree, may Allaah* *be pleased with him), Also the Messenger, may Allaah's praise and salutations be upon him, said, {**None of you truly believes until he loves for his brother that which he loves for himself.**} (Saheeh al-Bukharee :13 & Saheeh Muslim: 77)*

It is upon a person that he rectify himself firstly, and then turn to trying to rectify others from the direction of being someone who loves what is good for them and one who is sincere in conduct and advice towards them, but not doing so from the direction of simply diminishing others or indicating their faults and shortcomings without a Sharee'ah purpose. That would be something which Islaam prohibits him from doing, but doing so would be due to him being someone who loves goodness and rectification to reach those people.

In regard to a person saying, "This person is someone wicked," and "This other person is not like that". It is not justified in the Sharee'ah for one who is Muslim to state this in relation to the right of his Muslim brother except if that individual is clearly known for having turned away from what is correct, and is someone known for having an evil objective in what he does. In this case, then the one who knows the condition of such an individual it is obligatory upon him to say what he knows about his wickedness and him being far from what is correct, whenever doing so is based upon an established benefit for the religion. Such that he warns the people against that individual in order that they be protected from the danger he poses in what he does.

But for the individual who says this simply for the purpose of being able to obtain something in regard to that one, or simply to attack him without justification, then this is not permissible. This is simply personal animosity and disagreements, regarding which there is no clear established benefit for the Muslim in publicizing.

Moreover, there is no doubt that judging the specific states and conditions of individuals requires insight and the ability to verify and confirm. As a person cannot simply rely upon his suspicions or assumptions. Allaah, the Most High, says ❀**O you who believe! Avoid much suspicions, indeed some suspicions are sins. And spy not, neither backbite one another.**❀*-(Surah al-Hujuraat: 12)*

Similarly it is obligatory for a person that they do not rely upon what is conveyed or narrated from the reports of a wrongdoer or corrupt individual, as Allaah, the Most High, says: ❀**O you who believe! If a rebellious evil person comes to you with news, verify it, lest you harm people in ignorance, and afterwards you become regretful to what you have done.**❀*-(Surah al-Hujuraat: 6) For this reason, it is upon a person that they should avoid having unjustified evil suspicions about others and that they do not judge merely according to their personal suspicions.*

It is also upon him to not accept reports from those who bring them forward without careful examination and without confirmation of what is being conveyed, and that they do not make judgments about the people except through possessing the required Sharee'ah knowledge. And if he possesses the required Sharee'ah knowledge, then he judges, as is required, according to what he has examined and confirmed to be true. But if he is someone who does not have clear knowledge of the Sharee'ah rulings and guidelines, then it is not permissible for him to judge and assess the various actions of the people.

It is upon a person to not enter into these domains and areas in which they do not have the knowledge required for working within them. As Allaah the Most High said, ❖*And follow not (O man i.e., say not, or do not or witness not, etc.) that of which you have no knowledge (e.g. one's saying: "I have seen," while in fact he has not seen, or "I have heard," while he has not heard). Verily! The hearing, and the sight, and the heart, of each of those you will be questioned (by Allaah).*❖-(Surah al-Isra': 36) And Allaah the Most High said,❖*... and saying things about Allaah of which you have no knowledge.*❖-(Surah al-A'raf: 33)

Such that the one who does not have the required Sharee'ah knowledge must not put forth and produce judgments and rulings upon the people simply based on his suspicions or simply on his opinion or what he personally feels to be true. Rather what he must do is cease and stop doing any of this, because this matter is very dangerous. Since the one who accuses a believer of that fault which he does not actually have or described him with a description which he in truth is not characterized by, then this returns back to and strikes that false accuser. This is just as is mentioned in the hadeeth narration that if a person first accused is someone who does not actually deserve that bad description or accusation, then certainly that bad description returns back upon the one who originally stated it.

Likewise, it is not permissible for a Muslim to haphazardly say to his brother, "Oh you wrongdoer," or "You disbeliever," or "Oh wicked one,", or whatever is similar to that from evil descriptions. Allaah, the Most High, said: ❖*O you who believe! Let not a group scoff at another group, it may be that the latter are better than the former; nor let (some) women scoff at other women, it may be that the latter are better than the former, nor defame one another, nor insult one another by nicknames. How bad is it, to insult one's brother after having Faith [i.e. to call your Muslim brother (a faithful believer) as: "O sinner", or "O wicked", etc.]. And whosoever does not repent, then such are indeed dhaalimoon (wrong-doers, etc.).*❧-(Surah al-Hujjurat: 11)

It is obligatory upon a Muslim to preserve and protect himself from entering into these areas and situations. If he is someone with knowledge and insight, who has ability to accurately judge, then he must assess and judge himself firstly, and then turn towards the people afterwards. Likewise it is an obligation that he has deliberateness and confirms matters after investigating and verifying them, and not be someone who rushes quickly into such matters."

Some of this beneficial meaning has been narrated from the exemplary scholar from the Salaf, Muhammad Ibn Sireen, may Allaah have mercy upon him, in that he stated, [42]

"We used to say that the people who were quickest to be preoccupied with discussing the faults of others, were those with the most faults themselves."

A second supporting narration states,

"Those fearing Allaah are occupied from being preoccupied with other people's faults, but people with many faults themselves are quickest to discuss the faults of others".

---

[42]   as-Samt of Ibn Abee Dunya: pg. 104 and narrated by Abu Bakr ad-Denooree in al-Majlis wa Jawaahir al-Ilm: vol. 5 pg. 166

One of the central and repeated advices given by the noble sheikh in his responses to the different questions about personal challenges and issues in striving to live their lives as Muslims, is to focus and give true attention to the Qur'aan and every practice that enables us to benefit from its guidance. This is opposed to the damaging focus that some people wrongly have of focusing upon devised statements of dhikr or poetry written by Sufees, which is not a new form of misguidance. Indeed, many centuries ago, Ibn Taymeeyah, may Allaah have mercy upon him mentioned,[43]

> "...As such if a worshiper adopts some endeavors without a basis in the revealed Sharee'ah seeking to fulfill some of his requirements, then it is said that, to the degree that he consumes and takes on that other devised practice, then the desire he has for what actually comes from the Sharee'ah itself, and using it, weakens and is reduced.

> This contrasts with the one who correctly gives importance to, and focuses upon, what comes from the Sharee'ah. That person values that legislated matter, which he loves and which he benefits from, such that it truly fulfills his religion and directs his practice of Islaam towards being complete. For this reason it is seen that many of those who listen to these written poems, with the aim of seeking rectification and purification of their hearts, experience a weakness and deficiency in their desire to listen to the revealed Qur'aan."

Many times the sheikh advises with the recitation of the Qur'aan with careful contemplation. Indeed, Allaah the Most High, mentioned in the Qur'aan, ❦ *Do they not then consider the Qur'aan carefully? Had it been*

---

[43] Iqtidaa'a as-Siraat al-Mustaqeem: vol. 1 pg. 543

from other than Allaah, they would surely have found therein many contradictions.❊-(Surah an-Nisa': 82) The guiding scholar 'Abdur-Rahman as-Sa'dee, may Allaah have mercy upon him, said in his beneficial commentary an explanation of this verse.

"Here the Most High indicates His command to contemplate and carefully think about His Book, and what that means is to ponder, think and reflect about the various meanings which it contains, to think deeply about it, about both its fundamentals and the secondary matters from it, and everything its verses require and call to. This is because the careful consideration of the Book of Allaah is the key to the various areas of knowledge and different realms of understanding, and through which the conclusions leading to every form of good are reached, and every branch and domain of knowledge are derived, as well as it being that which leads to an increase in the emaan of one's heart while enabling the roots of the tree of faith to plant themselves deeply within it.

Through this careful contemplation, one comes to know who is the Lord Who must be worshiped, what perfect attributes He possesses, and what must be disassociated from Him of attributes which are deficient. Through this contemplation one comes to understand the clear way which guides someone towards Him, the characteristics of those people who are proceeding upon that way, and what they will receive when they reach him through submission and obedience. Through this contemplation one comes to understand those who are enemies of Allaah, from among its actual true enemies, as well as that related path which only leads to His punishment, the characteristics of those people who are proceeding upon that way, and the causes they have enacted for ending up with that punishment.

Likewise reflection and thinking about the verses of the Qur'aan increases a worshiper of Allaah in knowledge, deeds, and sound insight into matters. It is for this reason that doing so is something which Allaah commands, encourages, and which He informs the creation is from the reasons due to which He sent down the Qur'aan. Just as Allaah the Most Exalted mentioned, **This is a Book the Qur'aan which We have sent down to you, full of blessings that they may ponder over its verses, and that men of understanding may remember.** *-(Surah Saad: 29) And as Allaah the Most Exalted mentioned,* **Do they not then think deeply in the Qur'aan, or are their hearts locked up from understanding it?** *-(Surah Muhammad: 24).*

From the benefits gained from contemplating the Qur'aan is that through it a worshiper gains an increased degree of certainty and firm knowledge that it is indeed the Word of Allaah. This is due to him seeing that the different verses support and verify each other, and that they agree with each other in what they convey. Such that you will see the different rulings, narrated accounts, and types of information are repeated in various places and passages in the Qur'aan, yet all of them are in agreement and affirm each other without contradiction.

Through this, one understands the complete nature of the Qur'aan and that its origins are from the One Whose knowledge encompasses every single matter in creation. For this reason Allaah the Most High said, **Do they not then consider the Qur'aan carefully? Had it been from other than Allaah, they would surely have found therein much contradictions.** *-(Surah an-Nisa': 82) meaning that since it is from Allaah its essential nature is that it is free from any contradictions and errors."*

Ibn al-Qayyim, may Allaah the Most High, have mercy upon him, said,[44]

> *"If people understood what benefit could be found in the practice of reading and reciting the Qur'aan with careful contemplation they would occupy themselves with it rather than anything else. Such that if you are reciting, along with thinking carefully about the verses recited, then when you happen to come upon a verse which is about something you need to strengthen and rectify your heart, then you repeat it several times, perhaps even a hundred times, or to the degree of repeating it the entire night. As reciting a verse while thinking carefully about it and understanding its guidance is much better then completely reciting a large portion without contemplation and understanding. Moreover, it brings more benefit to the heart and it calls one toward the increasing of your emaan and tasting the sweetness of the Qur'aan.*
>
> *Doing this is what has been mentioned as the practice of the guided first generations of Muslims. One of them might continually repeat and focus upon a single verse until the morning prayer. Additionally, it is affirmed that the Messenger of Allaah, may the praise and salutations of Allaah be upon him, stood in ritual prayer reciting a single verse repeating it until the time of fajr. That verse was the statement of Allaah,* ❧ ***If You punish them, they are Your slaves, and if You forgive them, verily You, only You are the All-Mighty, the All--Wise .*** ❧*-(Surah al-Ma'idah: 118) Certainly, reciting the Qur'aan while thinking carefully about its guidance is the very foundation to the rectification of one's heart."*

This also benefits us in our efforts of memorization of the Qur'aan. It is narrated on the authority of Ibn 'Umar, may Allaah be pleased with both of them, that the Prophet, <u>may the praise</u> and salutations of Allaah be upon him,

[44] Miftaah Dar al-Sa'aadah, vol. 1 pg. 187

said,[45]

> *{When one who has committed the Qur'aan*
> *to memory (or who is familiar with it) gets up*
> *for night prayer and recites it night and day, it*
> *remains fresh in his mind, but if he does not get up*
> *(for prayer and thus does not recite it) he forgets*
> *it.}*

Ibn Taymeeyah, may Allaah have mercy upon him, summarized this ocean of benefits related to our turning our faces to focus upon the Qur'aan by saying,[46]

> *"I have not seen anything which nourishes the mind*
> *and the soul, which preserves one's physical body, and*
> *possesses what leads a worshiper to contentment more*
> *than the practice of continually and regularly reading*
> *and studying the guidance found within the Qur'aan,*
> *the Book of Allaah , the Most Glorified and the Most*
> *Exalted."*

There are also additional benefits which may come from a Muslim giving attention to the reading and recitation of the Qur'aan, which many might be unaware of, but which were mentioned by some of the people of knowledge from among the first distinguished generations of this Muslim Ummah. 'Abbaas Ibn 'Abdul-Daa'im al-Ma'ree al-Kinaanee, may Allaah have mercy upon him, said that Sheikh Dhareer advised and counseled him saying, [47]

> *"Frequently recite the Qur'aan and do not turn away*
> *from doing so, as this will facilitate and make easy*
> *for you that other knowledge which you are seeking,*
> *according to how often you recite the Qur'aan."*

> *He himself said, "So I've come to see that this is true*
> *and myself tested it and practiced it often. Whenever I*

---

[45] Saheeh Muslim: 789
[46] Majmu'a al-Fataawa vol. 7 pg. 493
[47] Dheel Tabaqaat al-Hanabilah: vol 2 pg. 98

would recite frequently it would generally be made easy for me to study and listen to hadeeth narrations and write down and record many of them. And if I did not recite the Qur'aan, then this other effort was not made easy for me."

In connection to their recitation, the leading scholars -past and present- were also diligent in considering the verses of the Qur'aan, writing down the understanding which that contemplation produced, as well as later teaching that to others. Sheikh Muhammad Ibn Saaleh al-'Utheimeen, may Allaah have mercy upon him, mentioned in his explanation of the work *al-Kaafeyah ash-Shaafeeyah* of Ibn al-Qayyim, about his well-known Sheikh and teacher,

"...I saw a small book which was possessed by Sheikh 'Abdur-Rahman as-Sa'dee, may Allaah have mercy upon him. He said it was his book in which during Ramadhaan when he was reciting the Qur'aan, whenever he came across a verse that called for it, he would stop at that verse, contemplate its meaning, and write down about its various benefits that occurred to him which were not found in the presently available works which explain the Qur'aan."

In relation to the efforts of the early scholars to teach the Qur'aan, Imaam adh-Dhahaabee, may Allaah have mercy upon him, mentioned in Seyar 'Alaam an-Nubalaa [48] that Sheikh al-Islaam Abu 'Ismaeel al-Harawee, may Allaah have mercy upon him, held three hundred and sixty sittings of knowledge explaining and understanding just the specific verse ❦*Verily those for whom the good has preceded from Us* ❧-(Surah al-Anbiyaa':101). This helps us understand why the Qur'aan should have such a place of priority in our lives and studies.

Furthermore, it also is the firm foundation for clarifying every form and type of misguidance and innovation found

[48] Seeyar 'Alaam an-Nubalaa vol. 18 pg. 514

among the Ummah, past and present. As Imaam Ahmad, may Allaah have mercy upon him, said, [49]

"If a person were to truly contemplate the Qur'aan, he would surely find that which refutes every individual upon innovation in the religion as well those new innovations those people proceed upon."

IMPORTANCE OF SUPPLICATION WHEN SEEKING RECTIFICATION AND STEADFASTNESS

Another of the central advices given by the noble sheikh in his responses to the different questions of those striving to rectify their lives as Muslims is to be diligent in the practice of supplicating to Allaah alone for assistance, rectification, steadfastness, and every good a believer needs. This is also something the Salafee scholars have always focused upon. Their works clarifying the importance of only directing supplication to Allaah alone rather than the forbidden practice of asking help from the righteous dead in graves, claiming to seek their intercession with Allaah for you. We should always remember and be encouraged by the fact that Allaah is the One who hears and can answer every single supplication directed sincerely to Him alone despite our state of sin and wrongdoing. Consider what Ibn 'Uyainah, may Allaah have mercy upon him, said,[50]

"Do not turn away from making supplication, do not allow what you know of your own faults to prevent you from making them. As certainly, Allaah answered the supplication of Iblees, and he is the most evil of all creation. **۞Iblees said: "Oh my Lord! Give me then respite till the Day they (the dead) will be resurrected. Allaah said: "Then verily, you are of**

---

[49] as-Sunnah of Khalaal pg. 912
[50] Shu'ab al-Emaan: vol. 1 pg. 53

those reprieved,❀-*(Surah al-Hijr: 36-37)"*

What is important is to establish the making of supplications in your daily life, as a regular practice based upon the guidance of the Sunnah. It is narrated on the authority of 'Umar Ibn al-Khattab, may Allaah be pleased with him, that he said, [51]

> *"Certainly I do not give any concern to the expected responses to my supplications, but give importance to making supplications. As when focusing upon making supplications then the desired response to them comes along with that."*

From the guidance of the Sunnah is purity of intention in everything we undertake, and this is truly important to remember when supplicating to Allaah. It is narrated on the authority of 'Abdullah Ibn Mas'ood, may Allaah be pleased with him, that he said, [52]

> *"Allaah only accepts the earnest and purest of supplications. Certainly He, the Most High, doesn't accept that which is made so that you are heard by others, nor that done for show and prominence, nor that done playing around, nor that made while being distracted or heedless. He only accepts that supplication made earnestly, sincerely from one's heart."*

This importance of sincerity becomes even more clear from what has been narrated on the authority of Hudhaifah, may Allaah be pleased with him, in that he said,[53]

> *"The people will soon reach a time in which no one will be successful in surviving its trials, except the person who makes supplications, the way a drowning man makes supplications to Allaah."*

---

[51] As narrated by Ibn Taymeeyah as transmitted in his work Iqtidhaa' as-Siraat al-Mustaqeem.

[52] Shu'ab al-Emaan: vol. 2 pg. 51-52

[53] This was narrated by Imaam al-Bayhaqee in Shu'ab al-Emaan: vol. 2 pg. 52 and Ibn Abe Shaybah in his Musannaf vol. 7 pg. 40

For this reason, making it our regular practice in all conditions opens the doors for a Allaah's assistance in the future. It has been narrated that Abu ad-Dardaa', may Allaah be pleased with him, said,[54]

"Supplicate to Allaah during those days in which you are in ease and things are going well, so that perhaps He may respond to your supplications during those days in which you face trials and difficulties."

Another matter for us all to remember, especially for someone working to make beneficial changes in their life, is that those good deeds you increase in when trying to better yourself as a Muslim can be a further reason for your supplications to be answered by Allaah. Imaam at-Tabaree narrates in an explanation of the statement of Allaah, the Most Glorified and the Most Exalted, ﴾ ***And your Lord said: "Invoke Me, and ask Me for anything I will respond to your invocation.*** ﴿-(Surah Ghaafir: 60) that al-Hasan al-Basree, may Allaah have mercy upon him, said,[55]

"Know with surety, and be given glad tidings, that it is a right of those who have faith in Him and do good works upon Allaah, the Most Glorified and the Most Exalted, that He respond to them and increase them in His favors."

Just as it has been narrated that the Companion Abu Dhar, may Allaah be pleased with him, said,[56]

"It is sufficient to make supplication along with a measure of engaging in good efforts, just as it is sufficient to have food along with a measure of salt."

---

[54] This was narrated by Imaam Ahmad in his work az-Zuhd pg. 135, Abu Na'eem in al-Hilyah: vol. 1 pg. 225, and Imaam al-Bayhaqee in Shu'ab al-Emaan: vol. 2 pg. 52

[55] Narrated by Imaam at-Tabaree, in his explanation of the Qur'aan vol. 2 pg. 94, and by at-Tabaraanee in his work ad-Duaa' pg. 9

[56] Ibn Abe Shaybah in his Musannaf vol. 7 pg. 40

So do not be like the one who supplicates for rectification of his shortcomings as a Muslim, but wrongly neglects other good deeds and personal efforts which would actually help bring that about, as Wahb bin Munabih said, [57]

> *"The one who supplicates without joining that with deeds and actions, is like the one trying to shoot an arrow without any bow".*

If you truly want rectification, no matter how many problems we have and how many issues we face in our personal lives, rectification is possible in this world and life. So we should always remember the essential role making supplication has always played in the life of the striving worshipers of Allaah. What an excellent statement is found from Habeeb Abee Muhammad who said, [58]

> *"The overall proven remedy and cure for matters is making supplication."*

IMPORTANCE OF AUTHENTIC DHKIR WHEN SEEKING RECTIFICATION AND STEADFASTNESS

A third important advice given by the noble sheikh in his beneficial responses to the different questions of those Muslims seeking rectification and closeness to Allaah, is to be regular in the practice of making dhikr as is found in the pure authentic Sunnah. Yet many of us, when we read about the authentic forms of dhikr mentioned in the treasured works in which the Sunnah has been preserved, are not fully aware of the important meanings within them from the direction of our essential beliefs as Muslims. In an excellent selection entitled 'The Sharee'ah

[57] Narrated by Ibn Abe Shaybah in his Musannaf vol. 7 pg. 39 and in Shu'ab al-Emaan: vol. 1 pg. 53
[58] Mujaabooa ad-Da'wah of Ibn Abee ad-Dunyaa

Objectives Of The Authentic Statements Of Dhikr', Sheikh Muhammad Baazmool explains to us that,[59]

"The different wording of the statements of dhikr found in the source texts are all related to four meanings:

Firstly, removing and freeing Allaah from evil, deficiency, or fault. This is the basis and fundamental meaning of subhanAllaah " (how free is Allaah from any fault or shortcoming).

Secondly, glorifying Allaah, the Blessed and the Most High, and praising Him. The basis of this is offering Him, the One free from all fault, praise, such as is found in the statement of remembrance "alhamdulillah" (all praise is due to Allaah)

Thirdly, supplicating for the sake of offering worship, or for the sake of turning to Allaah regarding a specific issue or request. The best of supplications and the best forms of dhikr or remembrance is the statement "La ilaha illa Allaah" (there is none worthy of worship except for Allaah). Moreover, this refers back to what is found in the various statements and forms of asking for forgiveness from Allaah, and of sending praise and salutation upon the Prophet, (may the praise and salutation of Allaah be upon him).

Fourthly, exalting and venerating Allaah. The basis of this is found in the statement "Allaahu akbar" (Allaah is the greatest) Since al-Kabeer is the One who is exalted far above everything other than Him. Meaning that Allaah is greater than everything and everyone. He is greater in His ability and Exalted nature. He is the One Whose greatness is due to His essential nature and perfect attributes. His position of greatness and grandeur is found in the hearts of His close associates from among

---

[59] As found from the Sheikh official Facebook pg.

both the people of the earth and the angels in the heavens.

These four meanings are found in all righteous beneficial statements of remembrance:

SubhanAllaah, alhamdulilah, Allaahu akbar, la ilaha illa Allaah (How free is Allaah from any fault or shortcoming, all praise is due to Allaah, Allaah is the greatest, there is none worthy of worship except for Allaah)

For this reason these four expressions are repeated in different forms in the various transmitted statements of remembrance.

All of these meanings are gathered in the phrase "al-hamd wa thinaa' lilllah 'aza wa jall" Since al-hamd, encompassing the meaning of freeing Him from all deficiencies, as well as that supplication made for the sake of offering worship, and the praising and exaltation of Him, who is free from every fault, in both His essential nature and His affirmed attributes.

For this reason, and Allaah knows best, it is mentioned in the hadeeth related to the major intercession of the Prophet for his Ummah on the Day of Reckoning. The Prophet suffices with that statementm which offers the praise of Allaah, as this praise itself encompasses every required meaning of dhikr and remembrance.

*This authentic narration was mentioned by al-Bukhaaree in the Book on Tawheed, in the nineteenth chapter "..**To one whom I have created with Both My Hands…**" as hadeeth number 7410 and also narrated by Imaam Muslim in the Book of Faith, in the chapter "**The Status of the Lowest people in Paradise**" hadeeth number 193*

*Additionally, from the hadeeth of Anas, may Allaah be pleased with him, which states, {... **I will then raise my head and praise my Lord with certain praises which He has taught me, and then I will intercede...}** and in the wording found in Saheeh Muslim {**I would then stand before Him and would extol Him with praises which I am not able to do now, but with which Allaah would inspire me.}***

Such that he, the Messenger, was the one who continually praised Allaah. As is mentioned in the Qur'aan, ❖**Glorified be your Lord, the Lord of Honor and Power! (He is free) from what they attribute unto Him! And peace be on the Messengers! And all the praise and thanks be to Allaah, Lord of the 'alameen (mankind, jinn and all that exists).**❖- *(Surah As-Saffaat: 180-182)"*

From among the beneficial narrations related to remembrance of Allaah, which some of the prominent past and present scholars of hadeeth have stated is authentic, is the following narration. It is a narration containing a statement of dhikr that should be relatively easy to use with little memorization or difficulty in learning, especially for some of our older brothers who have not had the opportunity to learn the Arabic language, as some of them have mentioned to me. The hadeeth is on the authority of `Amr bin Shu`aib who narrated from his father, from his grandfather, that the Messenger of Allaah said:

*{**Whoever says "subhanAllaah" (which means how free is Allaah from any fault or shortcoming) a hundred times before the rising of the sun and before its setting, it is better than one hundred sacrificial camels.***

And whoever who says "alhamdulillah" (which means all praise is due to Allaah) a hundred times before the rising of the sun and before its setting, it is better than providing a hundred horses in the cause of Allaah."

And whoever says "Allaahu akbar" (which means Allaah is the greatest) before the rising of the sun and before its setting, it is better than freeing a hundred slaves.

And whoever say "La ilaha illa Allaah wahdahu la shareek lahu, lahu al-mulk wa lahu alhamd wa hu alaa kulli shayan qadeer." (which means there in none worthy of worship except Allaah alone, having no partners. His is the dominion, and to Him belong all the praises and thanks, and He is able to do all things.) a hundred times before the rising of the sun and before its setting, then no one shall bring on the the Day of Resurrection, more than what he brought, except one who said similar to what he said, or increased upon it.[60]

How many authentic sound statements of dhikr which the Messenger of Allaah, may the praise and salutations of Allaah be upon him, taught directly to the best generation of Muslims, the Noble Companions, may Allah be pleased with them all, have some people left and turned away from. They have abandoned them, in order to adopt something newly developed and brought into the practices of Islaam, but unknown to the first and best Muslims whom emigrated to Medinah for Allaah's sake, and unknown to those from the Muslims of Medinah who supported them fully for Allaah's sake.

---

[60] Sheikh al-Albaanee authenticated this narration in his work Saheeh at-Targheeb wa al-Tarheeb no. 658 saying "Hasan (authentic) as narrated by an-Nasaa'ee." In the related footnote he states "Narrated by an-Nasaa'ee, meaning in the work 'al-Yawn wa Layl' (476/821) from the narrations of al-Awzaa'ee on the authority of 'Amr Ibn Shu'aib. I say this chain is hasan - an acceptable degree of authenticity and that al-Haafidh Ibn Hajr indicated his own strengthening of it in Fath al-Baaree: vol. 11: pg. 202.

The Companion's lived their lives upon the clear guidance of their beloved Prophet, and found sufficiency in what he conveyed to them from his Lord. They, may Allaah be pleased with them all, became successful in this life and the next by adhering closely to those specific beliefs, statements and actions which the Messenger of Allaah, may the praise and salutations of Allah be upon him, turned their heads towards, had them focus upon, and placed directly in their hands. Yet today, many wish to turn our heads in a different direction towards new beliefs and acts of worship that were completely unknown to those successful believing men and women. This is true whether that new focus be through the transgression of engaging in a new methodology of inner self improvement and rectification, or reviving and reinventing acts of varying levels of minor and major disbelief of seeking assistance, slaughtering animals for, and supplicating to the dead righteous in their graves, as practiced and called to by some extreme Sufees.

Many of the people today unfortunately have become accustomed to and feel safe heedlessly taking from these different directions, ideas, and programs when trying to better themselves and their lives. Yet we should actually slow down, stop and give them a long discerning look, always being aware that misguidance is something that is easy to slip into. This was true in the early century of Islaam when Shaytaan inspired people towards misguidance and it is true today. As is well known to many of us, one of the early scholars Imaam al-Barbahaaree, may Allaah have mercy upon him, said:

May Allaah have mercy upon you! Examine carefully the speech of everyone you hear from in your time particularly. So do not act in haste and

do not enter into anything from it until you ask and see: Did any of the Companions of the Prophet, may Allaah's praise and salutations be upon him, speak about it, or did any of the scholars? So if you find a narration from them about it, cling to it, do not go beyond it for anything and do not give precedence to anything over it and thus fall into the Fire.

Sheikh Saaleh al-Fauzaan, may Allaah preserve him, explained this statement saying, [61]

"Do not be hasty in accepting what you may hear from the people as correct, especially in these later times. As now there are many who speak about so many various matters, issuing rulings and ascribing to themselves both knowledge and the right to speak. This is especially the case after the emergence and spread of new modern day media technologies..."

Furthermore he, may Allaah preserve him, also emphasized in another work the danger of someone feeling that they don't need to be careful about slipping into clear misguidance in their personal understanding and practice of Islaam, saying, [62]

"No one should commend or praise himself in relation to his practice of his religion. No one should be someone who does not fear falling into trials and harmful circumstances, as long as they are still alive in this world. As every individual or person can be subjected or exposed to harmful trials. Indeed, well known prominent scholars have become misguided, and their steps faltered and they slipped into matters of falsehood, and so ended up upon misguidance. Yet these were people who were scholars!

---

[61] A Valued Gift for the Reader Of Comments Upon the Book Sharh as-Sunnah', pg. 102

[62]   E'aanat al-Mustafeed fee Shark Kitaab at-Tawheed vol. 1 pg. 129

Therefore the danger is significant and serious, and a person should never consider themselves safe from him possibly stumbling and tripping up in the affairs of the religion and so slipping into misguidance." '

But if we establish Islaam as the first Muslims did, by fulfilling the command to have taqwa in everything we do, we establish that firm foundation to practically rectify our lives, to truly purify our souls and be successful. Having taqwa, by fulfilling the commands of Allaah revealed in Islaam- as much as we can, and staying away from the prohibitions revealed in Islam, ensures that we follow Allaah's guidance inwardly and outwardly with falling into extremism or neglect. Sheikh al-Fauzaan, may Allaah preserve him and extend his life, explained this general command to strive and struggle to always have and act upon taqwa, saying the following, [63]

"....The one who fears Allaah to the limits of his capacity and ability, then he fears Allaah truly and properly as He should be feared. It is upon a Muslim to fear Allaah consistently and regularly in every place and location. He should fear Allaah in his situations of ease as well as when he is in difficulty and hardship. He should fear Allaah publicly when he is among the people, and fear Allaah when he acts privately away from them. This is just as was mentioned by the Prophet, may Allaah's praise and salutations be upon him, when he said, **{Fear Allaah wherever you are...}**

As for the person who fears Allaah publicly among the people but when he is in private he opposes Allaah by committing transgressions and wrongdoing, then this is the path travelled by the hypocrites who will be in the lowest levels of Hellfire, where they will find no one to assist or help them.

---

[63] Taken from a sermon found at http://www.alfawzan.af.org.sa/node/14392

But the believer strives to fear Allaah continually and consistently in a condition of hardship and one of ease and well being, in any place he might be, he is afraid of Allaah's punishment and fears him. This person is the one who fears Allaah correctly, so all of you must hold firmly to this essential matter of taqwa, may Allaah bless you all"...

So do not underestimate the true blessing of being guided to practice Islaam through establishing taqwaa as opposed to adopting a methodology of claimed special daily or weekly innovated gatherings or practices of dhikr. As one of the earlier scholars, Ja'far Ibn Muhammad, said,[64]

"The one whom Allaah, the Most Glorified and the Most Exalted, takes out of the dark shadow of disobedience to the glory and honor of obedience has been enriched without material wealth, and has been given comfort without it being necessary for a companion from among men to offer it to him, and has been made noble without a tribe to convey that upon him by lineage."

I advise myself and every striving Muslim to hold close to the people of the Sunnah and adherence to the Jama'ah, those who are truly satisfied with the Sunnah in every respect of their lives, and who are actually striving to make the Sunnah a reality in their lives and the lives of their families, despite all of our many shortcomings in that. Imaam Ahmad, may Allaah have mercy upon him, said towards the end of the letter which he is known to have sent to al-Mussadad,[65]

"...Love the people of the Sunnah upon what they might have among them. We ask that Allaah make you and us die upon the Sunnah and upon adherence to the Jamaa'ah, and that Allaah bless you and us that we truly follow knowledge, and that He bless you and us to stand upon whatever He loves and is pleased with of matters."

[64] al-Adaab as-Sharee'ah: pg.. 153
[65] Tabaqaat Al-Hanaabilah: vol. 1, pg. 345

This statement reminds us that the choosing of good companions is so essential to us as Muslims generally, and specifically, even more so for anyone who realizes that he must give importance and focus to self-rectification and growth as a Muslim, and start to give that importance. Certainly the Messenger, may Allaah's praise and salutation be upon him and his family, said, *{An individual is upon the religion of his associate or friend}* [66] Imaam Ibn al-Qayyim, may Allaah, the Most High, have mercy upon him, explains how that choice of associates and friends is actually reflected in our lives, [67]

"The person who is the most beneficial to you is the one who empowers and strengthens that good within yourself, such that it cultivates goodness within you and helps you produce and facilitate that which benefits you. Such a person is a blessed support for you in striving to benefit yourself, and just as you benefit from your interaction with him, in truth he benefits from his interaction with you, maybe even to a greater degree.

While the most harmful of people to you is the one who emboldens and strengthens that which is within you, such that you are directed to disobey Allaah, so he is someone who assists you in harming yourself and lowering yourself towards ruin."

We should each seek for ourselves and our true friends a successful good end to this passing life. And we must know, and should remind ourselves often, that this means dying firmly upon that straight path we have embraced as Muslims. Mu'tamir Ibn Sulaymaan, may Allaah have

---

[66] Narrated in Sunan Abu Daawud: 4833/ Jaame'a at-Tirmidhee: 2378/ & Musnad Imaam Ahmad: 7968, 8212/ -from the hadeeth of Abu Hurairah. It was declared authentic by Sheikh al-Albaanee in Silsilat al-Hadeeth as-Saheehah :927, Mishkaat al-Masaabeh: 5019, Saheeh al-Jaame'a as-Sagheer: 5858, his verification of al-'Emaan by Ibn Taymeeyah pg. 55, as well as in Saheeh Sunan Abu Dawud, & Saheeh Sunan at-Tirmidhee. Sheikh Muqbil declared it authentic in al-Jaame'a al-Saheeh: 4565, 4292.
[67] al-Fawa'id pg. 192

mercy upon him, from the early Muslims, said, [68]

> *"My father once came into where I was, where I was sitting depressed or sad. He asked me, "What is the matter?" I replied, "One of my friends has died."*

> *He then asked, "Did he die upon the Sunnah?" I answered "Yes." So he said, "Then do not worry or fear for him."*

Similarly, reminding us that our efforts to live Islaam are something we must be continually committed to until we leave this abode of tests and trials. Imaam Ahmad, may Allaah have mercy upon him, said, [69]

> *"The one who dies upon Islaam generally, and the Sunnah specifically, dies upon every form of good."*

That good end is what we must strive for as the true goal as a Muslim seeking steadfastness upon the truth. Muhammad Ibn Hasnaweeyah, from the early Muslims, narrates,[70]

> *"I was sitting in the presence of Abu 'Abdullaah Ahmad Ibn Hanbal when a man came to him from the people of Khurasaan. The man said, 'Oh Abu 'Abdulllah I came to you from Khurasaan specifically to ask you about an important matter. Imaam Ahmad said to him. "Ask." So then the man said, "When does the worshiper of Allaah come to taste the assurance and comfort in his efforts of life?"*

> *Imaam Ahmad, said. "When he is blessed to take his first step into Jannah."*

This is accomplished through gaining the true closeness with Allaah in the next world, which people of the Sunnah seek, by adhering closely to the revealed guidance

---

[68] Sharh Usul 'Itiqaad Ahlus-Sunnah of Imaam Laalakaa'ee vol.1 pg. 67

[69] Siyaar 'Alaam an-Nubalaa' vol. 11 pg. 296

[70] Tabaqaat Al-Hanaabilah vol 1. pg. 291

of Islaam and turning away from all other inferior ways in this world. The guiding scholar Sheikh Zayd Ibn Muhammad al-Madkhalee, may Allaah the Most High, have mercy upon him, explains the reality of that final success of true blessed closeness to Allaah by saying, [71]

"When Allaah reveals Himself, in a manner which suits His majesty, to His close associates in Jannah, they will forget every incredible blessing and reward that have been given until that time.

Oh Allaah, do not forbid from us the good that is with You of Your favor and goodness due to that evil and those wrongs that we ourselves have of shortcomings and transgressions, this we ask You, the Most Generous, the Most Gracious, the Most Merciful."

I close saying, as the noble distinguishing and cultivated sheikh the guiding scholar Sheikh Ahmad Ibn Yahya an-Najmee, may Allaah have mercy upon him, stated in his introduction to the book *'Al-Fataawa al-Jaleeyah'* part 2,

"I do not free myself from committing mistakes in this work, as indeed no one is free of this. And I hope from the noble reader that if he encounters something that it is obligatory to warn about that they should draw my attention to that as someone whom indeed I would thank, and that they inform me of that mistake, clarifying to me what exactly is the mistake in what was stated and how it conflicts with Sharee'ah evidences. As the brother who advises me will find me as one who submits and yields to the truth, turning towards it.

That which I do request from the reader is that they offer supplications for me in my absence. As indeed I am in need of such supplications, that Allaah forgive my sins, and that He give me insight into my shortcomings, and that He bless me with steadfastness upon the truth until I meet Him as one clinging even to the very edges of the Sunnah, having proceeded

[71] Awdhah al-Ma'anee pg. 189

upon the straight methodology and way, and having placed my reliance upon the Most Gracious, the Most Merciful."

That which is correct from my efforts as a student is from the guidance of Allaah and only through His mercy, and that which is deficient is only from myself and Shaytaan, the accursed enemy of those who believe.

We ask Allaah guide us towards every action of true self rectification that He is pleased with, and distance us from every false priority, focus, and undertaking, which may cause us fall into one of the traps of Shaytaan.

May the praise and salutations of Allaah be upon the Messenger of Allaah, his household, his Companions, and all those who follow his guidance until the Day of Judgement. All praise is due to Allaah alone, Lord of all the worlds.

Abu Sukhailah Khalil Ibn-Abelahyi
Taalib al-Ilm Educational Resources
the 3rd of Shawwal, 1438

(Corresponding to Jun 27th, 2017)

(1)

SEVEN GOALS & OBJECTIVES WHICH ARE SOUGHT AFTER THROUGH LEARNING AND AFFIRMING THE CORRECT BELIEFS OF ISLAAM

The true basis of rectification of every human being lies in firstly affirming the correct beliefs about the Creator in order to worship Him alone, and then about the creation in order to fulfill Allaah's various commands in relation to it. Towards this goal it truly benefits each of us, as striving Muslims, to get a better understanding of the overall and wider objectives which the beliefs of Islaam call for, and truly produce by Allaah's permission.

A brief yet concise explanation of these objectives which sound beliefs direct to is found in final pages of the beneficial work '*Explanation of the Fundamentals of Emaan*', by the guiding scholar Sheikh Muhammad Ibn Saaleh al-'Utheimeen, may Allah have mercy upon him, as found below.[1] It is a strong encouragement for each of us to ensure that our beliefs are correct by being built upon the foundations of the Qur'aan and authentic Sunnah.

"The word goal (or objective) in the Arabic language generally has several meanings, from them is "a matter which is aimed at in order to hit or reach it," and "every object or matter which is intended and sought after."

The goals which are sought after by establishing the correct beliefs of Islaam within people, meaning the objectives of affirming the correct beliefs and the noble goals which are sought after by means of adhering to those correct beliefs, are numerous and of different kinds. From among them are:

Firstly: attaining a pure and sincere intention in establishing the worship of Allaah, the Most High, alone. This is because He is the Creator, who has no associate, therefore it is required that He be the object of our intention and that every form of worship be directed to Him alone, without any partner in that.

---

[1] This was taken from the Dar al-Watan printing- first edition 1410, only the title has been slightly modified.

Secondly: liberating of the mind and one's thoughts from the presence of different chaotic and mixed up ideas, beliefs, and concepts that naturally are produced when someone's heart lacks these firm sound beliefs. This is because the person whose heart does not have within it the foundation of the sound beliefs of Islaam is either: empty and hollow lacking any clear beliefs at all, such that he only directs his worship, attention, and focus towards material matters and physical sensual experiences, or his beliefs are corrupted and confused due to being affected by various false beliefs and baseless superstitions mixed within them.

Thirdly: instilling and developing true personal contentment and peace of mind within someone, so that within himself he finds overall peace and within his various thoughts he is not conflicted and unstable. The sound beliefs of Islaam establish the correct and proper relationship between a believer and the One who created him, such that he comes to be pleased with Allaah as his commanding Lord and legislating Judge. Furthermore, it leads the believer to be comfortable and accepting of Allaah's decrees within his heart, and within himself he finds acceptance and full contentment with Islaam, without having a need to look to anything else to replace it.

Fourthly: safeguarding of both one's inward intentions and their outward actions from deviating and turning away from guidance in whatever they put forth of worship to Allaah, the Most High, or within how they interact and deal with Allaah's created beings. This is because one of the central pillars of the correct beliefs is the belief in the sending of the messengers to humanity with revelation, and this belief encompasses and includes following their way and path which brings about soundness in both a believer's intentions and deeds.

Fifthly: facilitating and promoting being resolute and committed in one's affairs as a Muslim. Such that someone does not see an opportunity for good except that he steps forward and utilizes it for righteous deeds, hoping for Allaah's reward in doing so, and likewise he does not see a situation of wrongdoing and harm except that he moves away from it and distances himself from it fearing that it may lead him to the punishment of Allaah. Because one of the central pillars of the correct beliefs is the belief in the eventual resurrection of humanity and them all being compensated for their deeds -good or bad. Allaah says, ❖*For all there will be degrees (or ranks) according to what they did. And your Lord is not unaware of what they do*❖-(Surah al-An'aam: 132). The Prophet, may the praise and salutations of Allaah be upon him, himself encouraged this objective as found in his statement, *{The strong believer is better and more beloved to Allaah than the weak believer, although within both is good. Strive for that which will benefit you, seek the help of Allah, and do not feel helpless. If any hardship reaches you, do not say, "If only I had done such and such" rather say "Allah has decreed and does whatever He wills." For saying, 'If...' opens the door to the actions of Shaytaan}* (Saheeh Muslim: 1988, Sunan Ibn Maajah: 79).

Sixthly: establishing a strong Muslim Ummah that will do whatever is required, and pay the needed price, to properly establish its religion and correctly reinforce and strengthen its pillars and foundation, without having any concern for the harms and difficulties they encounter while preceding upon the path of carrying this out. Regarding this Allaah , the Most High, has said, ❖*Only those are the believers who have believed in Allaah and His Messenger, and afterward doubt not but strive with their wealth and their lives for the Cause of Allaah. Those! They are the truthful.*❖-(Surah al-Hujjarat:13)

Seventh: achieving success and contentment in both this worldly life and the Hereafter through rectifying individuals and societies, gaining both Allaah's reward and honor from Him. Regarding this, Allaah, the Most High, has said,

❦ *Whoever works righteousness – whether male or female – while he (or she) is a true believer verily, to him We will give a good life (in this world with respect, contentment and lawful provision), and We shall pay them certainly a reward in proportion to the best of what they used to do (i.e. Paradise in the Hereafter).* ❧-(Surah an-Nahl: 97).

These are some of the goals and objectives which are sought after through learning and affirming the correct beliefs of Islaam. I pray and hope that Allaah the Most High will enable their realization for us here, and for all of the Muslims."

(2)

WE MUST TAKE ADVANTAGE OF WHAT REMAINS OF OUR LIVES, TO RETURN BACK TO ALLAAH...[1]

---

[1]   This title was taken from the text itself not the original audio file.

It is upon us to scrutinize and look carefully at what we've done within the first half of the month of Ramadhaan that has passed. If what we put forth is efforts of good, then for that we praise Allaah, and we must increase and expand that. And if it was not good then we must repent to Allaah, the Most Glorified and the Most Exalted, and make up for it by utilizing the remainder of the month before it passes away.

This is what is obligatory upon a Muslim, that they do not continue upon their heedlessness, focusing upon the things that are not beneficial. That they do not simply proceed along with the people and whatever the people proceed upon of heedlessness and focusing upon that which is not beneficial. Rather one must take notice and be mindful of this, and each will inevitably become mindful eventually. That recognition of the importance of how one's time was spent will inevitably come when death reaches him. There is no doubt that he will recognize it then, but is it possible for him to repent from his heedlessness at the point of death? No, it is not possible at that time. So one must take notice and recognize this while he is still among those who are living, and while he is still able to repent from heedlessness. Otherwise, when he reaches that inevitable recognition which comes when a person dies, then he can only be regretful, regretting his lost opportunities.

If he was someone who was righteous, then he will regret that he did not increase upon the good which he did. And if he was someone who was not righteous, then he will certainly regret his life because of what he wasted, foolishly spent it upon, and allowed of his life to pass by in what was of no true value. And there is no strength to

[2]   Taken from an audio file in the voice of the esteemed Sheikh

change from one state to another, from good to evil, except through Allaah. So it is upon all of us, upon every Muslim, that we truly turn back fully to Allaah, the Most Glorified and the Most Exalted -that we take stock and fully assess what occurred in our time which has passed, and that we ask for Allah's forgiveness in what we have fallen short in during the period which has gone by. Allaah, the Most Glorified and the Most Exalted, will forgive all of our sins; certainly He is the Most Forgiving, the Most Beneficent.

RETURN

We ask Allaah, the Most Glorified and the Most Exalted, to grant us success to be upon righteous statements and deeds, and that He make us and you from those who fast this month and receive its full and complete reward, and successfully obtain for ourselves the reward from our Lord the Most Perfect and the Most High. That being a reward which is not comparable to anything else, a reward only given by our Lord. As for the recompense or rewards of this worldly life, or that which is received from other people, then it is both something which passes away as well as that which can put you to trial. But the reward from our Lord, the Most Perfect and the Most High, is the true recompense and reward.

It is the reward which comes about for the one who sacrifices and who puts forth efforts in what causes and leads to this reward within his life and throughout his years. Throughout the time he has and within every moment, during his days and his months, and over the course of his entire life, he puts forth the effort to bring what causes the achievement of this reward. This cause is: righteous deeds and endeavors; turning in repentance to Allaah, the Most Glorified and the Most Exalted; engaging in many good efforts; and repenting from the evil that we do. This is what achieves this reward, by Allaah's permission.

However, we must remember that this success lies within the hand of Allaah, the Most Glorified and the Most Exalted, remembering that Allaah is the Most

Exalted, the Most Magnificent, is All-Wise, All-Knowing, Who places every matter in its proper place. He is the One who gives this reward to the one who deserves it, and prevents it from being obtained by the one who does not truly deserve it. Certainly He is the One who is the most knowledgeable of the conditions of those who worship Him amongst His creation. As such, it is upon us to have vigilance and give true attention to ourselves and where we stand.

We must take advantage of what remains from our time within this month of Ramadhaan. Moreover we must take advantage of what remains of our lives, to return back to Allaah, the Most Glorified and the Most Exalted, repenting from our lapses and transgressions as Muslims. Additionally it is upon us to rectify our actions and endeavors, to rectify ourselves, to rectify our children, and rectifying those situations that we find around us. This is what is obligatory upon us all. And it is Allaah who grants success and is the One who guides to the right path. May the praise and salutations of Allaah be upon our Prophet, upon his family, and all his Companions.

(3)

BENEFITS CONNECTED TO HAVING TAQWA IN THIS WORLD & THE NEXT[1]

---

[1]   This work has a total of forty-six points combined in two sections and was published by Dar al-Qaasim. It is, in fact, a different publication from, and not a summary of, a similar work published by the Sheikh al-'Utheimeen Foundations with a similar title which consists of one hundred and eighteen points in a single section.

All praise is due to Allaah, Lord of all the worlds, may the salutations of Allaah be upon the noblest of messengers our Prophet Muhammad, and upon his household, and all his Companions. As for what follows:

My believing brothers and sisters, what Allaah has enjoined upon all of His worshipers from the early and later times is to have fear, or taqwa, of Him Who is the Most Perfect and the Most High. Certainty, Allaah, the Most High and the Most Exalted, said: *And to Allaah belongs all that is in the heavens and all that is in the earth. And verily, We have recommended to the people of the Scripture before you, and to you (O Muslims) that you (all) fear Allaah, and keep your duty to Him, But if you disbelieve, then unto Allaah belongs all that is in the heavens and all that is in the earth, and Allaah is Ever Rich (Free of all wants), Worthy of all praise.*-(Surah An-Nisaa': 131)

This is also what the Messenger of Allaah, may the praise and salutations of Allaah be upon him, advised his Ummah. As is narrated by Abu Umaamah Sadaa Ibn 'Ajlaan al-Baahalee, I heard the Messenger of Allaah, may the praise and salutations of Allaah, be upon him, say *{Have Taqwa of your Lord, and pray your five ritual prayers, and fast your month, and pay the zakaat on your wealth, and obey those who are in charge of you, you will enter the Paradise of your Lord.}* (Jaame'a at-Tirmidhi: 616)

Furthermore, whenever he would dispatch someone to travel to complete some task, who was to act as a leader in charge of a group of Muslims going with them, he would specifically advise him that he should act with, and proceed upon, taqwa of Allaah in his undertaking, and to treat those Muslims under his authority in the best way. The righteous Muslims of the first three generations never

---

[2] From 'Summarized Responses to Ten Questions' transcribed from the voice of the sheikh

ceased advising the Muslims with this in their sermons, their writings, and their advice to the worshipers at the time of their deaths.

'Umar Ibn al-Khattab wrote to his son 'Abdullah, "*As for what follows: Indeed I advise you to have taqwa, or fear Allaah, the Most Glorified and the Most Exalted, as certainly you will eventually meet Him, and you have no one Who prohibits matters other than Him, and He is the One who possesses the dominion of this worldly life and the Hereafter.*"

Someone known to be from among the early righteous people wrote in a letter to one of his Muslim brothers saying, "*As for what follows: I counsel and advise you to have taqwa of your Lord, who is the unseen confidante in each of your private affairs, and the observer in every one of your outward affairs. As such, make Allaah the one who is prominent in your heart and mind in every situation of how you spend your day and your night. Fear Allaah to the degree of His certain closeness to you and His undeniable power over you. Know that you are under His two eyes, and that you cannot escape from His authority towards some other authority, nor can you escape from His dominion to stand under some other dominion. Therefore, glorify Him by truly acting with caution in everything you undertake, and increase in your fear and apprehension of His punishment. As-salaam.*"

The meaning of taqwa is: for a worshiper of Allaah to place a barrier or protection between himself and what he fears of punishment, and place himself behind it. Such that the Muslim worshiper having taqwa of his Lord means: that he place a barrier between himself and that which he fears of his Lord's anger and wrath, in which he can protect himself from that, and this is through performing acts of obedience and through staying away from acts of disobedience and wrongdoing.

Additionally, respected Muslim brother, there are also other statements from our righteous predecessors which further make clear and understandable the meaning of taqwa. Ibn 'Abbaas, may Allaah be pleased with them both. said, *"The people of taqwa are those who act upon their fear of Allaah and His punishment."*

Talq Ibn Habeeb said, *"Taqwa is to act in obedience to Allaah upon light given by Allaah, hoping and seeking the reward of Allaah, and to turn away from engaging in sins and transgressions against the commands of Allaah, upon light given by Allaah, fearing the punishment of Allaah."*

Ibn Mas'ood, may Allaah be pleased with him, said in explaining, ❧**O you who believe! Fear Allaah as He should be feared...**❧-(Surah al-Imraan: 102) "That you obey Allaah and not disobey Him, that you remember Allaah and not forget about Him, that you are grateful and thankful to Allaah and that you do not deny or disbelieve." [3]

So be attentive, my respected brother, to having taqwa of Allaah, the Most Glorified and the Most Exalted. As Allaah , how free from any imperfection is He, is the one most deserving of being feared and exalted and of being held as tremendous and almighty in your heart. The following is, for you, an explanation of some of the benefits connected to you acting with and having taqwa.

---

[3] Narrated authentically in this form back to the Companion in Tafseer Ibn Jareer vol.4 page 19, and al-Mustradrak of al-Hakim: vol.2 page 294, who said "authentic upon the conditions of al-Bukhaaree and Muslim", and Imaam adh-Dhahabee agreed with his assessment. This is as mentioned by Sheikh al-Albaanee who commented after narrating these sources, "..And it is as these scholars have mentioned" in Silsilat al-Hadeeth as-Saheehah vol. 14. page 955 narration number 6906

Firstly: Benefits Connected to You Having Taqwa In this World

1- Having taqwa is the cause of things generally being made easier for someone. Allaah, the Most High, said: ❧ *...and whosoever fears Allaah and keeps his duty to Him, He will make his matter easy for him.* ❧-(Surah at-Talaaq: 4) And Allaah, the Most High, said: ❧ *As for him who gives (in charity) and keeps his duty to Allaah and fears Him. And believes in Al-Husna. We will make smooth for him the path of ease (goodness).* ❧-(Surah al-Layl: 5-7)

2- Having taqwa is the cause of being protected from the harm of Shaytaan. Allaah, the Most High, said: ❧ *Verily, those who have taqwa when an evil thought comes to them from Shaytaan , they remember Allaah, and indeed they then see aright.* ❧-(Surah al-A'raaf: 201)

3- Having taqwa is the cause of Allaah sending down blessing from both heaven and the earth. Allaah, the Most High, said: ❧ *And if the people of the towns had believed and had the taqwa (piety), certainly, We should have opened for them blessings from the heaven and the earth, but they belied (the Messengers)* ❧-(Surah al-A'raaf: 96)

4- Having taqwa is the cause of a worshiper being blessing with the ability to successfully distinguish between the truth and falsehood, and properly understand them. Allaah, the Most High, said: ❧ *O you who believe! If you obey and fear Allaah, He will grant you Furqaan a criterion [(to judge between right and wrong...* ❧-(Surah al-Anfal: 29) And Allaah, the Most High, said: ❧ *... Fear Allaah, and believe too in His Messenger (Muhammad), He will give you a double portion of His Mercy, and He will give you a light by which you shall walk (straight), ...* ❧-(Surah al-Hadeed: 28)

5- Having taqwa is the cause of being given a way out of difficulties, and being given sustenance and an increase in one's livelihood from unexpected directions for the one who fears Allaah. Allaah, the Most High, said: ❁ *And whosoever fears Allaah and keeps his duty to Him, He will make a way for him to get out (from every difficulty). And He will provide him from (sources) he never could imagine. And whosoever puts his trust in Allaah, then He will suffice him. Verily, Allaah will accomplish his purpose. Indeed Allaah has set a measure for all things.* ❁ -(Surah At-Talaaq: 2-3)

6- Having taqwa is the cause of gaining the level of being the pious worshipers of Allaah, as certainly the close associates of Allaah are those who have fear or taqwa of Him. Just as Allaah, the Most High, has said: ❁ *And why should not Allaah punish them while they stop (men) from al-Masjid-al-Haraam, and they are not its guardians? None can be its guardian except those who have taqwa...* ❁ -(Surah al-Anfal: 34) Moreover, Allaah, the Most High, said: ❁ *Verily, the Zaalimoon (polytheists, wrong-doers, etc.) are protectors and helpers to one another, but Allaah is the Walee (Helper, Protector, etc.) of those who have taqwa.* ❁ -(Surah al-Jaathiyah:19)

7- Having taqwa is the cause of not being afraid of being harmed by the schemes and plans against you by the disbelievers. Allaah, the Most High, said: ❁ *But if you remain patient and become those who have taqwa, not the least harm will their cunning do to you. Surely, Allaah surrounds all that they do.* ❁ -(Surah al-Imraan: 120)

8- Having taqwa is the cause of having groups of assisting angels sent down from the heavens during confrontations, in order to also face your enemies alongside you. Allaah, the Most High, said: ❁ *And Allaah has already made you victorious at Badr, when you were a weak little force. So fear Allaah much that you may be grateful. (Remember) when you (Muhammad) said to the believers, "Is it not enough for you that your Lord (Allaah)*

should help you with three thousand angels; sent down?"
"Yes, if you hold on to patience and piety, and the enemy
comes rushing at you; your Lord will help you with five
thousand angels having marks of distinction.❱-(Surah al-
Imraan: 123-125)

Through this sending down of groups of supporting
angels, the Muslims receive glad tidings, the believers'
hearts are blessed with satisfaction, and they are granted
victory from Allaah the All-Mighty, the All-Wise. Just as
Allaah, the Most High, said: ❰*Allaah made it not but as*
a message of good news for you and as an assurance to your
hearts. And there is no victory except from Allaah, the All-
Mighty, the All-Wise.❱-(Surah al-Imraan: 126)

9- Having taqwa leads to preventing enmity and
causing harm between the worshipper of Allaah, as Allaah
has said, "*....Help you one another in al-birr and at-taqwa*
(virtue, righteousness and piety); but do not help one
another in sin and transgression. And fear Allaah.❱-(Surah
al-Ma'idah: 2). And Allaah, the Most High, said in the
account of Maryam, ❰*She placed a screen (to screen herself)*
from them; then We sent to her Our Ruh [angel Jibrael], and
he appeared before her in the form of a man in all respects.
She said: "Verily! I seek refuge with the Most Beneficent
(Allaah) from you, if you do fear Allaah.❱-(Surah Maryam:
17-18)

10 - Having taqwa is the cause of someone honoring
and esteeming the symbol or distinctive hallmarks of the
religion of Allaah. Allaah, the Most High, said: ❰*And*
whosoever Honors the Symbols of Allaah, then it is truly
from the piety of the heart.❱-(Surah al-Hajj: 32)

11 - Having taqwa is the cause of having our endeavors
and actions rectified and accepted by Allaah, as well as
having our sins and wrongdoing forgiven by Allaah.
Allaah, the Most High, said: ❰*O you who believe! Keep*
your duty to Allaah and fear Him, and speak (always) the
truth. He will direct you to do righteous good deeds and
will forgive you your sins. And whosoever obeys Allaah and

His Messenger he has indeed achieved a great achievement (i.e. he will be saved from the Hell-fire and made to enter Paradise).-(Surah al-Ahzaab:70-71)

12 - Having taqwa is the cause of the worshiper properly lowering his voice when with the Messenger of Allaah, whether this was done during his life in his presence, or after his death when near his grave. Allaah, the Most High, said: *Verily! Those who lower their voices in the presence of Allaah's Messenger, they are the ones whose hearts Allaah has tested for piety. For them is forgiveness and a great reward.*-(Surah al-Hujuraat: 3)

13 - Having taqwa is the cause of gaining Allaah's love of you, the Most Glorified and the Most Exalted is He. This love from Him will be in this world just as it will also be in the next life. This is just as mentioned in the authentic qudsee narration where the Messenger of Allaah, may the praise and salutations of Allaah be upon him, said that Allaah says, *{I will declare war against him who treats with hostility a pious worshipper of Mine. And the most beloved thing with which My slave comes nearer to Me, is what I have enjoined upon him; and My slave keeps on coming closer to Me through performing voluntary prayers or doing extra deeds besides what is obligatory until I love him. So much so that I become his hearing with which he hears, and his sight with which he sees, and his hand with which he strikes, and his leg with which he walks; and if he asks Me something, I will surely give him, and if he seeks My Protection or refuge, I will surely protect him}* (Saheeh al-Bukhaaree: 386) And just as Allaah, the Most High, said: *Yes, whoever fulfils his pledge and fears Allaah much; verily, then Allaah loves those who are those who have taqwa.*-(Surah al-Imraan: 76)

14 - Having taqwa is the cause of acquiring and gaining knowledge. Allaah, the Most High, said: *So have taqwa of Allaah; and Allaah teaches you. ...*-(Surah al-Baqarah: 182)

15 - Having taqwa is the cause of the one having it being better protected from going astray or becoming misguided after Allaah had blessed him to stand upon guidance. Allaah, the Most High, said: *And verily, this is my Straight Path, so follow it, and follow not other paths, for they will separate you away from His Path. This He has ordained for you that you may become Those who have taqwa* -(Surah al-An'am: 153)

16 - Having taqwa is the cause of receiving the mercy of Allaah upon you. This mercy from Him will be in this world just as it will also be in the next life. Allaah, the Most High, said: *....and My Mercy embraces all things. That Mercy I shall ordain for those who are those who have taqwa , and give Zakaat; and those who believe in Our Ayaat (proofs, evidences, verses, lessons, signs and revelations, etc.* -(Surah al-A'raaf: 156)

17 - Having taqwa is the cause of gaining a way of being with Allaah that is specific and special. This is since the way Allaah is with His worshipers is of two separate types. Firstly there is the general being with them, this includes all of His worshipers, by means of His hearing, seeing, and complete knowledge. Certainly, Allaah is the All-Hearer, All-Seer, and All-Knowing of every situation and condition of those worshipers. Allaah, the Most High, said: *And He is with you (by His Knowledge) wheresoever you may be. And Allaah is the All-Seer of what you do.* -(Surah al-Hadeed: 4)

And Allaah, the Most High, said: *Have you not seen that Allaah knows whatsoever is in the heavens and whatsoever is on the earth? There is no najwa (secret counsel) of three, but He is their fourth (with His Knowledge, while He Himself is over the Throne, over the seventh heaven), nor of five but He is their sixth (with His Knowledge), not of less than that or more, but He is with them (with His Knowledge) wheresoever they may be...* -(Surah al-Mujaadilah: 7)

As for the second type, it is a specific meaning of His being with some of those worshipers. This type encompasses granting them assistance towards victory, supporting them and helping them succeed. Allaah, the Most High, said: ❀*...and he said to his companion (Abu Bakr): "Be not sad (or afraid), surely Allaah is with us.*❀- (Surah al-Tawbah: 40)

And Allaah, the Most High, said: ❀*He (Allaah) said: "Fear not, verily! I am with you both, hearing and seeing.*❀- (Surah Ta-Ha: 46)

There is no doubt that the specific form of being with Allaah is granted for those of His worshippers who have taqwa. Allaah, the Most High, said: ❀*Truly, Allaah is with those who fear Him (keep their duty to Him), and those who are muhsinoon*❀-(Surah An-Nahl:128)

And Allaah, the Most High, said: ❀ *...And fear Allaah, and know that Allaah is with Those who have taqwa*❀-(Surah al-Baqarah: 194)

18 - Having taqwa is the cause of reaching a good end and conclusion to one's life and efforts. Allaah, the Most High, said: ❀*And the good end (i.e. Paradise) is for those who have taqwa*❀-(Surah Ta-Ha: 132) And Allaah, the Most High, said: ❀*...and verily, for those who have taqwa is a good final return (Paradise)*❀-(Surah Saad: 49) And Allaah, the Most High, said: ❀ *Surely, the (good) end is for those who have taqwa*❀-(Surah Hud: 49)

19 - Having taqwa is the cause of being given good tidings during this worldly life, whether this be directly through a true dream of your own or of others which contains good tidings of something, or by a separate means of being blessed to have the people love you and praise your good efforts. Allaah, the Most High, said: ❀*Those who believed (in the Oneness of Allaah - Islamic Monotheism), and used to fear Allaah much (by abstaining from evil deeds and sins and by doing righteous deeds). For them are glad tidings, in the life of the present world (i.e.*

righteous dream seen by the person himself or shown to others), and in the Hereafter. No change can there be in the Words of Allaah, this is indeed the supreme success.❧-(Surah Yunus:63-64)

Imaam Ahmad narrated on the authority of Abu ad-Dardaa' narrated from the Prophet, may Allaah's praise and salutations be upon him, regarding the statement of Allaah, ❧*For them are glad tidings, in the life of the present world ...*❧-(Surah Yunus: 63-64) "This means a true dream which they see themselves, or someone righteous sees regarding them."

Similarly, on the authority of Abu Dharr that he said, *{Oh Messenger of Allaah, what do you say about a man who strives in doing good deeds, such that the people come to praise him due to this. He replied, "This is from those good tidings for a believer which he has received in this world."}*

20 - When Muslim women have taqwa and implement its causes for maintaining goodness, which includes not being soft in speech with unrelated men, their keeping away from this ends up being what prevents those who have some sickness in their heart from having desires stirred up in the hearts when interacting with those women. Allaah, the Most High, said: ❧*O wives of the Prophet! You are not like any other women. If you keep your duty (to Allaah), then be not soft in speech, lest he in whose heart is a disease (of hypocrisy, or evil desire for adultery, etc.) should be moved with desire, but speak in an honorable manner.*❧-(Surah al-Ahzaab: 32)

21 - Having taqwa is the cause of being preventing from being excessive when making a bequest to others before death, separate from the inheritance he leaves. Allaah, the Most High, said: ❧ *It is prescribed for you, when death approaches any of you, if he leaves wealth, that he make a bequest to parents and next of kin, according to reasonable manners. (This is) a duty upon those who have taqwa* ❧-(Surah al-Baqarah: 180)

22 - Having taqwa is the cause of giving women who have been divorced but are in their 'iddah period their due financial maintenance during this period before the divorce is finalized. Allaah, the Most High, said: *And for divorced women, maintenance should be provided on reasonable scale. This is a duty on those who have taqwa.* - (Surah al-Baqarah: 241)

23- Having taqwa is the cause of not losing the reward of your deeds in this world or the next. Allaah, the Most High, said after blessing the prophet Yousef, may Allaah salutations be on him, by reuniting him with his blood brothers after their separation: *Verily, he who fears Allaah with obedience to Him (by abstaining from sins and evil deeds, and by performing righteous good deeds), and is patient, then surely, Allaah makes not the reward of the muhsinoon (good-doers) to be lost.* -(Surah Yusuf: 90)

24- Having taqwa is the cause of truly receiving guidance from Allaah due to it. Allaah, the Most High, said: *Alif-Lam-Meem. This is the Book (the Qur'aan), whereof there is no doubt, a guidance to those who have taqwa [the pious and righteous persons who fear Allaah much (abstain from all kinds of sins and evil deeds which He has forbidden) and love Allaah much (perform all kinds of good deeds which He has ordained)].* -(Surah al-Baqarah:1-2)

Secondly: Benefits Connected to You Having Taqwa In the Next World

1- Having taqwa is the cause of ultimately gaining a position of honor with Allaah , the Most Glorified and the Most Exalted. Allaah, the Most High, said: ❴*Verily, the most honorable of you with Allaah is that (believer) who has At-Taqwa [i.e. one of those who have taqwa].*❵-(Surah al-Hujuraat: 13)

2- - Having taqwa is the cause of ultimate success and true salvation. Allaah, the Most High, said: ❴*And whosoever obeys Allaah and His Messenger , fears Allaah, and keeps his duty (to Him), such are the successful ones.*❵-(Surah An-Nur: 52)

3 - Having taqwa is the cause of being saved on the Day of Resurrection from Allaah's punishment. Allaah, the Most High, said: ❴*There is not one of you but will pass over it (Hell); this is with your Lord; a Decree which must be accomplished. Then We shall save those who use to fear Allaah and were dutiful to Him. And We shall leave the polytheists and wrongdoers, therein humbled to their knees (in Hell).*❵-(Surah Maryam: 71 -72). And Allaah, the Most High, said: ❴*...And those who have taqwa will be far removed from it (Hell).*❵-(Surah al-Layl: 17)

4- Having taqwa is the cause of Allah accepting and rewarding you for your works and various good deeds. Allaah, the Most High, said: ❴*Verily, Allaah accepts only from those who have taqwa.*❵-(Surah al-Ma'idah: 27)

5- Having taqwa is a strong cause of gaining the inheritance of Jannah. Allaah, the Most High, said: ❴*Such is the Paradise which We shall give as an inheritance to those of Our slaves who have been those who have taqwa.*❵-(Surah Maryam: 63)

6- The people of taqwa will receive the reward of incredible rooms or chambers built on top of each other in Jannah. Just as Allaah, the Most High, said: *But those who fear Allaah and keep their duty to their Lord (Allaah), for them are built lofty rooms; one above another under which rivers flow (i.e. Paradise). (This is) the Promise of Allaah: and Allaah does not fail in His Promise.*-(Surah Az-Zumar: 20)

'Ali narrated that the Messenger of Allah said:

{Indeed in Paradise there are chambers whose outside can be seen from their inside, and their inside can be seen from their outside." A Bedouin stood and said: "Who are they for Oh Prophet of Allah?" he said: "For those who speak well, feed others, fast regularly, and perform ritual salaat for Allaah during the night while other people sleep.} (Jaame'a at-Tirmidhi: 2527)

7- Taqwa is the cause of those having it to be protected and shielded on the Day of Judgement from its chaos. They will be far above those disbelievers, who in their horrible state of crowded confusion and fear are fruitlessly moving around in pitiful throngs of people. But the people of taqwa will have a settled location many degrees above them among those believers resting in highest of positions. Allaah, the Most High, said: *Beautified is the life of this world for those who disbelieve, and they mock at those who believe. But those who obey Allaah's Orders and keep away from what He has forbidden, will be above them on the Day of Resurrection. And Allaah gives (of His Bounty, Blessings, Favors, Honors, etc. on the Day of Resurrection) to whom He wills without limit.*-(Surah al-Baqarah: 212)

8- Having taqwa is the cause of being made to enter into Paradise. This is due to the fact that Paradise has been prepared for them. Allaah, the Most High, said: *And march forth in the way (which leads to) forgiveness from your Lord, and for Paradise as wide as are the heavens and the earth, prepared for those who have taqwa.*-(Surah al-Imraan: 133)

And Allaah, the Most High, said: *And if only the people of the Scripture (Jews and Christians) had believed in Muhammad and warded off evil (sin, ascribing partners to Allaah) and had become those who have taqwa. We would indeed have blotted out their sins and admitted them to Gardens of pleasure in Paradise.*-(Surah al-Ma'idah: 65)

9- For those who have taqwa it is the cause for their evil actions being wiped away and their mistakes to be excused in the Hereafter. Allaah, the Most High, said: *... and whosoever fears Allaah and keeps his duty to Him, He will remit his sins from him, and will enlarge his reward.*-(Surah At-Talaaq: 5) And Allaah, the Most High, said: *"And if only the people of the Scripture (Jews and Christians) had believed in Muhammad and warded off evil (sin, ascribing partners to Allaah) and had become those who have taqwa. We would indeed have blotted out their sins and admitted them to Gardens of pleasure in Paradise.*-(Surah al-Ma'idah: 65)

10- Having taqwa is the cause of, ultimately, those who are Muslim gaining whatever they desired and delights their eyes as rewards. Allaah, the Most High, said: *'Adn (Eden) Paradise (Gardens of Eternity) which they will enter, under which rivers flow, they will have therein all that they wish. Thus Allaah rewards those who have taqwa.*-(Surah An-Nahl: 31)

11- Having taqwa is the cause of the removal of fear and grief of the Day of Resurrection and to not be affected by the evil of that day. Allaah, the Most High, said: *And Allaah will deliver those who are those who have taqwa to their places of success (Paradise). Evil shall touch them not, nor shall they grieve.*-(Surah Az-Zumar: 61). And Allaah, the Most High, said, *No doubt! Verily, the close associates or auliyaa' of Allaah [i.e. those who believe in the Oneness of Allaah and fear Allaah much (abstain from all kinds of sins and evil deeds which he has forbidden), and love Allaah much (perform all kinds of good deeds which He has ordained)], no fear shall come upon them nor shall they grieve. Those who believed (in the Oneness of Allaah - Islamic Monotheism), and used to fear Allaah much (by abstaining from evil deeds and sins and by doing righteous deeds).*-(Surah Yunus: 62-63)

12- Those who have taqwa will be resurrected and come to Allaah as an honorable delegation or wafd. A wafd is a group or delegation that arrives while riding; they will be the best type of delegations to Allaah. Allaah, the Most High, said: *The Day We shall gather those who have taqwa unto the Most Beneficent (Allaah), like a delegate (presented before a king for Honor).*-(Surah Maryam: 85)

Ibn Katheer brought forth a narration from an-Nu'man Ibn Sa'ad in which he stated, "We were sitting with 'Alee and he recited the verse "*The Day We shall gather those with Taqwa unto the Most Gracious (Allah), like a delegation.*-(Surah Maryam: 85) He then said, *No by Allaah they will not be gathered on their feet, the delegation will never be gathered and proceed on their feet. Rather they will be gathered on she-camels the like of which mankind has never seen, on which are saddles of gold. They will ride them until they knock at the gates of Paradise.*" [4]

13- For those who have taqwa it is a cause of Jannah being brought closer to them in the Hereafter. Allaah, the Most High, said: *And Paradise will be brought near to those who have taqwa*-(Surah Ash-Shu'ara': 90)" And Allaah the Most High also said: *And Paradise will be brought near to those who have taqwa not far off.*-(Surah Qaaf: 31)

14- Having taqwa is the cause of being considered distinguished from others and not treated equal to the disbelievers and wrongdoers. Allaah, the Most High, said: *Shall We treat those who believe (in the Oneness of Allaah Islamic Monotheism) and do righteous good deeds,*

---

[4]   This narration is found in the Musnad of Imaam Ahmad: 1302, with a weak chain of narration, as mentioned in the modern verification of the Musnad of Imaam Ahmad by Sheikh Shu'aib al-Arnaut, who declared it weak and also mentioned some of its other related narrations in different sources with the same weak chain of narration. And Allaah knows best.

as Mufsidoon (those who associate partners in worship with Allaah and commit crimes) on earth? Or shall We treat those who have taqwa , as the criminals, disbelievers, and wicked?"-❧-(Surah Saad: 28)

15- Every companionship and friendship established for other than Allaah's sake will be overturned on the Day of Resurrection, except for the companionship established among the people of taqwa. Allaah, the Most High, said: ❧*Friends on that Day will be foes one to another except those who have taqwa.*❧-(Surah Az-Zukhruf: 67)

16 - Those who have taqwa will be given a place of security, entrance into Gardens, beautiful companions, and other tremendous rewards. Allaah, the Most High, said: ❧*Verily! Those who have taqwa, will be in place of Security (Paradise). Among Gardens and Springs; Dressed in fine silk and (also) in thick silk, facing each other, So (it will be), and We shall marry them to houris (female fair ones) with wide, lovely eyes. They will call therein for every kind of fruit in peace and security; They will never taste death therein except the first death (of this world), and He will save them from the torment of the blazing Fire,*❧-(Surah Ad-Dukhaan: 51-56)

17 - Those who have taqwa will be blessed with a seat of truth -meaning Paradise, near Allaah, the Omnipotent King. Allaah, the Most High, said: ❧*Verily, those who have taqwa will be in the midst of Gardens and Rivers (Paradise). In a seat of truth (i.e. Paradise), near the Omnipotent King (Allaah, the All-Blessed, the Most High, the Owner of Majesty and Honor).*❧-(Surah al-Qamar: 54-55)

18- Those who have taqwa will be blessed with rivers of different wonderful types in Jannah. One river has water whose taste is preserved and pure. Another will be of milk that doesn't sour or spoil. Another will be of pure wine which is delicious to all those who drink it. Allaah, the Most High, said: ❧*The description of Paradise which those who have taqwa have been promised is that in it are rivers of water the taste and smell of which are not changed;*

rivers of milk of which the taste never changes; rivers of wine delicious to those who drink; and rivers of clarified honey (clear and pure) therein for them is every kind of fruit; and forgiveness from their Lord...-(Surah Muhammad: 15)

Also it is mentioned in an authentic narration of the Messenger of Allaah, may the praise and salutations of Allaah be upon him, *{..so if you ask Allah for anything, ask Him for the Firdaus, for it is the last part of Paradise and the highest part of Paradise, from it spring forth the rivers of Paradise, and above it there is the Throne of Beneficent,...}* (the meaning of a narration in Saheeh al-Bukhari: 7423)

19 - Those who have taqwa will be in Jannah, blessed to be able to travel beneath the trees of Jannah, and sit comfortably beneath their shade. Allaah, the Most High, said: *Verily, those who have taqwa shall be amidst shades and springs. And fruits, such as they desire. Eat and drink comfortably for that which you used to do.*-(Surah al-Mursalaat: 41-43) Likewise on the authority of Anas Ibn Maalik who reports that the Messenger of Allaah , may the praise and salutations of Allaah be upon him, said, *{In Paradise there is a tree which is so big that a rider can travel in its shade for one hundred years without passing it}* -(Saheeh al-Bukhaaree: 4881)

20- Those who have taqwa will be given glad tidings in the Hereafter that they will not experience the terror of the Day of Reckoning, by those angels who will meet and convey this to them. Allaah, the Most High, said: *No doubt! Verily, the close associates or auliyaa' of Allaah, and love Allaah much (perform all kinds of good deeds which He has ordained), no fear shall come upon them nor shall they grieve. Those who believed, and used to fear Allaah much by abstaining from evil deeds and sins and by doing righteous deeds.   For them are glad tidings, in the life of the present world, and in the Hereafter. No change can there be in the Words of Allaah, this is indeed the supreme success.*-(Surah Yunus: 62-64)

Imaam Ibn Katheer, said, "As for these glad tiding in the Hereafter, then it is as Allaah the Most High stated: *"The greatest terror (on the Day of Resurrection) will not grieve them, and the angels will meet them with the greeting: "This is your Day which you were promised.*-(Surah al-Anbiyaa': 103)"

21- The people of taqwa are blessed with the best of homes in the Hereafter- Paradise. Allaah, the Most High, said: *For those who do good in this world, there is good, and the home of the Hereafter will be better. And excellent indeed will be the home (i.e. Paradise) of those who have taqwa*-(Surah an-Nuh: 30)

22- The people of taqwa are blessed with a doubling of the reward and recompense in the Hereafter. Allaah, the Most High, said: *Oh you who believe. Fear Allaah, and believe too in His Messenger (Muhammad), He will give you a double portion of His Mercy, and He will give you a light by which you shall walk (straight), and He will forgive you. And Allaah is Oft-Forgiving, Most Merciful.*-(Surah al-Hadeed: 28) "*a double portion*" meaning a double reward.

And Allaah, the Most High, knows best. May the peace and salutations of Allaah be upon our Prophet Muhammad and upon his family, and his Companions, all of them.

TAQWA

(4)

GUARDING OURSELVES & OUR FAMILIES FROM THE DANGERS WITHIN MODERN MEDIA

Howerver it is obligatory that we undertake the responsibility of developing our youth, of sheltering and supervising them wherever they go and during their travels, trips, and their vacations. Such that we just don't abandon them to do whatever they like, but knowingly raise them up upon the correct sound beliefs, within our schools, within our homes, and in our libraries and offices, and every other similar place.

We should never forget to give the needed attention to guiding them towards living their lives upon goodness. We cannot simply entrust this to someone else, leave them to do as they wish, having an unjustified confidence in them that they will do well without us working to surround them with that which will benefit them, and us working and struggling to protect them or prevent from them whatever harmful things might reach them.

For if we do not undertake this, then our youth will gradually slip into corruption and different forms of misguidance, just as others from among our Muslim Ummah around the world have slipped into misguidance. It is not enough that we simply say, "but our children are within our homes," because these calls and invitations and the individuals making them are now able to reach them directly within our very homes while they are sitting there within in our own houses.

For this reason, it is an obligation upon us that we give clear attention to this matter, and that we do not heedlessly abandon our youth to wherever they may go and whatever they may find on the Internet and these other media. Rather it is required that we manage them in <u>what they are d</u>oing and supervise them.

[1] A question posed after the lecture 'Warning the Muslim Youth Against the Biased Inviters'

FAMILIES

Additionally, we must discuss, clarify, and encouragingly call and convince them to understand that much of what is being directed towards them is actually something purposefully harmful to them and never intended to benefit them. Rather it is something which will undoubtedly harm them, and something which stands opposed to what they were raised upon as Muslims. They should know this, that it is intended to weaken and corrupt the blessings of Islaam within them."

He, may Allaah preserve him, also said, [2]

"...This is just as is apparent to most about those trials and different societal evils which are surging and spreading throughout the world today, which are not restricted only to the people directly involved or the original places they are found. No, they creep in being conveyed by various media. There are many different types of media which spread these evils which now reach and connect directly to a person sitting in their home, in the smallest area of their own house, except for the one who Allaah's mercy prevents this from.

It is for us to be warned against the trials coming to us and that we clean and free our houses from them, and that we prevent them from reaching and affecting our families and everyone who we are responsible for. As this is an open conflict, an offensive invasion against us, by which they are waging a war within our own homes while they fight against our families and against our children. Indeed Allaah says, ﴾*O you who believe! Ward off from yourselves and your families a Fire (Hell) whose fuel is men and stones, over which are (appointed) angels stern (and) severe, who disobey not, (from executing) the Commands they receive from Allaah, but do that which they are commanded.*﴿ -(Surah At-Tahreem: 6)

[2] Audio lecture 'Balance and Moderation in Islaam and Combatting Extremism'

This destructive fire storm of harm is entering your very own home, and it can ruin your children and your close relatives! So safeguard your house from it, since no one else has true control over what you allow to enter your home other than you, no one is able to rightly dispute with you in this. Even to the point of fact that the ruler is not able to control your home or do what he wishes in it! Your home is under your control and under your authority; no one else truly knows what is really happening there except for you. As such you are fully responsible for everything within your home.

So we must all fear Allaah, the Most Perfect and the Most High, regarding what goes on in our homes and regarding our children. We must be diligent in offering advice between ourselves as Muslim brothers, and between our neighbors in relation to those matters going on around and among us. We should act with love and mercy, with the offering of sincere advice and proper cooperation upon goodness and the fear of Allaah.

In this matter I ask Allaah for success for myself and for you, by means of having beneficial knowledge and putting forth righteous deeds, and having a sincere intention for Allaah, the Most Glorified and the Most Exalted, in everything that we say and do and in everything that we believe in our hearts. May the praise and salutations of Allaah be upon our Prophet Muhammad and upon his family, and all his Companions"

In response to a question from the same lecture, the Sheikh , may Allaah preserve him, said,[3]

"Parents are responsible for their children, responsible for protecting them from being exposed to harmful concepts and potentially adopting corrupt ideas, as well

[3] Audio lecture 'Balance and Moderation in Islaam and Combatting Extremism'

as from them having bad companions. They must be protected and defended against these things. Consider that if a person has a flock of sheep, wouldn't he work hard to keep them in a safe place and protect them from any wolf, or from a pack of wolves, or from thieves! So considering this, we ask: are someone's sheep more valuable and precious to him than his own children?!?

Therefore, firstly give priority to initially safeguarding your children, to protecting your children from those evil concepts and harmful ideas. Remove those means or mechanisms which bring in evil from the various forms of media such as satellite and digital media channels from your house. Remove them from your house, don't bring anything other than media which is good into your home, good media which actually benefits everyone.

Some examples of this are good lectures and advices, audio of reciters in their recitation of the Qur'aan, and general recordings of the sittings with the people of knowledge. And there are many beneficial things available, all praise is due to Allaah. But keep those corrupting forms of media and harmful things and sources far away from your houses - don't allow them to enter your homes. Certainly your homes are in the authority of your own hands, and you are able to control and manage them...."

Likewise the Sheikh , may Allaah preserve him, said, [4] "As for our youth, it is an obligation that we protect them, that we safeguard them from these newly-arriving ideas which bring corruption with them, these misguiding concepts and philosophies which are being spread and directed towards them while they sit quietly at home at the computer, or on their phones while they are in our cars.

---

[4]   A question after the lecture 'Hold close to the Legitimate Muslim Authority and the Guiding Scholars'

Today it is not proper nor acceptable that we are negligent about this issue. In fact it is an obligation that we proceed now to prevent this possible harm in a beneficial way by Allaah's permission. We undertake this starting initially with the children within our own homes, then it further expands to include working with those teachers within our schools, and then further includes those giving sermons in our masjids, and those leading the ritual prayer within them. All of them have a role in establishing what is needed to shelter and safeguard our Muslim youth.

And we must do what is necessary to guide them, and clarify these different things which are available to them which are intentionally directed against them. As certainly, the enemies of Islaam have not ceased working and cooperating to try to affect and influence our Muslim youth.

This is because they understand that the very pillar of this Muslim Ummah is its youth. They understand and truly comprehend that if they can influence and corrupt the minds of our youth, that this will lead to the breakdown and degeneration of the Muslim Ummah. And there is no strength nor power to change from one state to another except in Allaah.

So it is an obligation that we neither forget nor dismiss that there is a specific plan and overall agenda of the disbelievers. Furthermore, confronting this issue, it is not something which is removed from us individually. No, in fact everyone has a responsibility for this. Everyone must establish his obligation regarding this. If he is someone with some authority then he should use his authority, and if he lacks authority he must bring this issue to the responsible people of authority from among the Muslims, and bring these matters to the specific people responsible.

He cannot simply push it to someone else and delegate this responsibility into someone else's hands. Each and every one of us has a responsibility in regard to safeguarding ourselves and safeguarding our Muslim youth"

(5)

AN OVERVIEW OF THE BOOK
"HIGH ASPIRATIONS OR GOALS:
THOSE MATTERS WHICH STRENGTHEN
IT AND THOSE WHICH PREVENT IT"

Introduction by the Honorable Sheikh 'Abdul-Azeez Ibn Baaz

"All praise is due to Allaah, may the praise and salutations of Allaah be upon the one after whom there was no prophet sent.

To proceed:

Indeed I read the book "High Aspirations or Goals: Those Matters Which Strengthen It And Those Which Prevent It" by its author, the noble Sheikh Muhammad Ibn Ibraheem al-Hamd, and found it to be a beneficial book which encourages and assists towards doing good deeds and endeavors, as well as preventing against the commission of evil actions.

It encourages cooperation upon goodness and the fear of Allaah, and cooperation upon the truth while being patient upon it. So may Allaah bless him with goodness, increase his reward, and benefit the Muslims with this book of his. Certainly, Allaah is the One who gives bounty and is truly generous.

May Allaah's salutations be upon our Prophet Muhammad, his household, and his Companions.

The Head Scholar for Issuing Rulings for the Kingdom of Saudi Arabia

Head of the General Council of Major Scholars

Head of the Permanent Committee of Scholastic Research & Issuing of Islamic Rulings

Sheikh 'Abdul-'Azeez Ibn 'Abdullah Ibn Baaz,

ASPIRATIONS

Translated Table of Contents:

13. Distress about past misfortune and so abandoning new efforts and beneficial works

14. Excessive blaming of others and putting forth very little action yourself

15. Frequently complaining to other people

16. To have a strong want for something but a weak dedication to working for it

17. Procrastination and delaying of your efforts

18. To take pride in one's successful children living in their accomplishments instead of producing one's own

19. Excessive joking and becoming engrossed in humor

20. To be discouraged from rectification ever actually occurring

21. Begging and regularly asking of others' wealth despite being capable

22. Acting with pride and self-superiority

23. Being in the habit of lying and deceiving

24. Having little modesty in general

25. Harboring spite and excessive ill will towards others

26. Keeping company with foolish and crude people

27. Seeking out others' mistakes and being pleased when they slip or have a shortcoming

1. Someone's natural disposition towards not growing and progressing

2. Shortcomings in someone's early home education

3. Shortcomings in someone's environment and society

4. The scarcity of distinguished educators and model teachers to look towards around them

5. The negative effects of different forms of media

6. Someone being burdened by the difficulties of having a wife and children

7. Lack of encouragement from others

8. Companionship with evil people and association with those who in fact should be abandoned

9. Weakness of faith or emaan

10. Weakness of one's concern for the truth and what is connected to that

11. Being amazed by oneself and deeds

12. Seeking advice from the ignorant and from those who should be avoided and abandoned

13. Indecision and uncertainty in one's thoughts

14. Someone being excessive in his or her low opinion of themselves

15. Exaggeration in having fear of failure

16. Overly restricting one's scope of activity and focus

17. Exaggerated zeal and enthusiasm in a matter beyond what is proper

18. Exaggeration seeking perfection in matters

19. Having little patience while the path to success is long

20. Having too many endeavors and areas of work and focus

21. Wrongly making up excuses

22. Failing to act modestly in what you do

23. Having lack of fairness or justice in your endeavors

24. Jealousy towards what others have

25. Being greedy and avaricious of gathering wealth

26. Unrestricted general blind following of others

27. Illegitimate separating and differing with other Muslims

28. Having mistaken understandings in one's beliefs generally

29. Having mistaken understandings specifically about Allaah's decree

30. Being influenced by foreign belief systems and ideologies other than Islaam

Book 2

Preface: Is it possible to adopt and take on having high aspirations and goals?

Chapter 1: About having high aspirations

First section: The merits of high aspirations, the praise for it, and the encouragement to take on having them.

Second section: About high aspirations and noble goals

Third section: The position of Islaam towards having high aspirations

Fourth section: Radiant statements regarding high aspirations

Chapter 2: The reasons, or causes, for the adoption of or taking on high aspirations

1. One's natural disposition towards this

2. The effects of one's parents and their role in your gaining a sound education

3. Coming from a society that has many noble righteous people

4. Having respect for the leading scholars and being

ASPIRATIONS

under the care of competent individuals

5. The presence of distinguished educators and model teachers for someone

6. General encouragement towards high aspirations

7. Receiving sound guidance and acting in accordance with one's good disposition

8. Good effects from beneficial media

9. The soundness of one's fundamental beliefs

10. Striving in the path of Allaah

11. Having strong faith in Allaah the Most Glorified and the Most Exalted

12. Supplications made for success

13. Having modesty in one's affairs

14. Reading of the Qur'aan with contemplation and careful consideration

15. Knowledge of the historical events and periods the Muslims have encountered

16. Personal events and incidents that one passes through and benefits from

17. Turning away from living in luxury and comfort

18. The practice of determining things carefully and giving each matter its proper place

19. The practice of consulting those active intelligent people and avoiding consulting the foolish and those with few efforts

20. The practice of accepting constructive criticism and taking on purposeful good advice

21. Putting forth efforts based upon having a pure intention for Allaah's sake alone

22. A person's individual strength and vigor

23. The matter of generosity:

– the effect of generosity upon the dominance, the strength, of the Muslim Ummah

– from the different types of generosity

– the types of superiority people have in relation to their generosity

24. Keeping away from ignorant people

25. Acting with forgiveness, pardoning others, and dealing with injuries in the best of ways

26. To act humbly in one's life

27. Adherence to fairness in your dealings with others

– those matters which assists in ensuring someone acts with fairness and justice

28. Holding to being truthful and having personal parity and being far away from hypocrisy and being deceitful

29. The rejection of injustice in affairs

30. Having truthful care or strong concern for what is correct

31. Properly restricting one's worldly hopes and remembrance of the next life in the hereafter

32. Looking towards those that are better than you religiously in good qualities and deeds as well looking towards those who are of a lesser position than you in worldly affairs

33. Continually referring back to the guidance of the life history of the Prophet Muhammad

34. The reading and study of the life histories of the many Muslim heroes, righteous individuals, and distinguished personalities from among the believers

35. Traveling in and passing through the many different lands and benefiting from what one sees from an Islamic perspective

36. Consulting those who are rightly in positions of responsibility among the Muslims

37. Companionship with righteous people and those with high aspirations and goals

38. Trusting Allaah, along with seeking or utilizing the means to achieve one's goals and aspirations

39. To be optimistic and have a positive outlook generally

40. To be satisfied and generally pleased with one's life while continually seeking increase in good and betterment

41. To have patience inwardly, reflect patience in your affairs, and persevere in striving towards good

42. Establishing oneself on moderation and balance in both good times and bad times

43. To be diligent in taking some form of benefit from every person and situation that you encounter and deal with

44. The awakening of high aspirations inwardly and the stimulation of one's desire for it

45. The strengthening of one's desire towards achieving good and struggling against one's soul

46. Seizing the opportunities that one encounters

47. To maximize your time and get the most out of it

– from those matters which help you get the most of your time

48. Striving to be kept away from self-deception and excessiveness in looking down upon other people

49. Having fortitude and determination while not giving value towards the matter of being fearful

50. To be established upon accepting whatever benefits you and rejecting everything that does not

Section 3: Excellent examples of those with high aspirations

1. Nurruddeen Mahmood

    – Firstly his characteristics and virtues

    – Secondly his Jihaad, military victories, and reformations among the Muslims

    – Nurruddeen's example in relation to matters

2. Sheikh al-Islaam Ibn Taymeeyah

    – His knowledge

    – His worship

    – His method, guidance, and general character

    – His bravery and courage

3. The esteemed Sheikh Muhammad Ibn Ibraheem Aal-Sheikh

    – A summary of his life

    1. His being occupied with teaching and instructing Sharee'ah knowledge

    2. His praiseworthy character and personal characteristics

    3. His humility with Allaah

    4. His works, general endeavors, and activities

Conclusion: My Prayers, Wishes And Hopes

THE NAKHLAH EDUCATIONAL SERIES:

MISSION

The Purpose of the 'Nakhlah Educational Series' is to contribute to the present knowledge based efforts which enable Muslim individuals, families, and communities to understand and learn Islaam and then to develop within and truly live Islaam. Our commitment and goal is to contribute beneficial publications and works that:

Firstly, reflect the priority, message and methodology of all the prophets and messengers sent to humanity, meaning that single revealed message which embodies the very purpose of life, and of human creation. As Allaah the Most High has said,

❨ *We sent a Messenger to every nation ordering them that they should worship Allaah alone, obey Him and make their worship purely for Him, and that they should avoid everything worshipped besides Allaah. So from them there were those whom Allaah guided to His religion, and there were those who were unbelievers for whom misguidance was ordained. So travel through the land and see the destruction that befell those who denied the Messengers and disbelieved.* ❩–(Surah an-Nahl: 36)

Secondly, building upon the above foundation, our commitment is to contributing publications and works which reflect the inherited message and methodology of the acknowledged scholars of the many various branches of Sharee'ah knowledge who stood upon the straight path of preserved guidance in every century and time since the time of our Messenger, may Allaah's praise and salutations be upon him. These people of knowledge, who are the inheritors of the Final Messenger, have always adhered closely to the two revealed sources of guidance: the Book of Allaah and the Sunnah of the Messenger of Allaah- may Allaah's praise and salutations be upon him, upon the united consensus, standing with the body of guided Muslims in every century - preserving and transmitting the true religion generation after generation. Indeed the Messenger of Allaah, may Allaah's praise and salutations be upon him, informed us that, *{ A group of people amongst my Ummah will remain obedient to Allaah's orders. They will not be harmed by those who leave them nor by those who oppose them, until Allaah's command for the Last Day comes upon them while they remain on the right path. }* (Authentically narrated in Saheeh al-Bukhaaree).

The guiding scholar Sheikh Zayd al-Madkhalee, may Allaah protect him, stated in his writing, 'The Well Established Principles of the Way of the First Generations of Muslims: It's Enduring & Excellent Distinct Characteristics' that,

"From among these principles and characteristics is that the methodology of tasfeeyah -or clarification, and tarbeeyah -or education and cultivation- is clearly affirmed and established as a true way coming from the first three generations of Islaam, and is something well known to the people of true merit from among them, as is concluded by considering all the related evidence.

What is intended by tasfeeyah, when referring to it generally, is clarifying that which is the truth from that which is falsehood, what is goodness from that which is harmful and corrupt, and when referring to its specific meanings it is distinguishing the noble Sunnah of the Prophet and the people of the Sunnah from those innovated matters brought into the religion and the people who are supporters of such innovations.

As for what is intended by tarbeeyah, it is calling all of the creation to take on the manners and embrace the excellent character invited to by that guidance revealed to them by their Lord through His worshiper and Messenger Muhammad, may Allaah's praise and salutations be upon him; so that they might have good character, manners, and behavior. As without this they cannot have a good life, nor can they put right their present condition or their final destination. And we seek refuge in Allaah from the evil of not being able to achieve that rectification."

Thus the methodology of the people of standing upon the Prophet's Sunnah, and proceeding upon the 'way of the believers' in every century is reflected in a focus and concern with these two essential matters: tasfeeyah or clarification of what is original, revealed message from the Lord of all the worlds, and tarbeeyah or education and raising of ourselves, our families, and our communities, and our lands upon what has been distinguished to be that true message and path.

The Roles of the Scholars & General Muslims In Raising the New Generation

The priority and focus of the 'Nakhlah Educational Series' is reflected within in the following statements of Sheikh al-Albaanee, may Allaah have mercy upon him:

"As for the other obligation, then I intend by this the education of the young generation upon Islaam purified from all of those impurities we have mentioned, giving them a correct Islamic education from their very earliest years, without any influence of a foreign, disbelieving education."

(Silsilat al-Hadeeth ad-Da'eefah, Introduction page 2.)

"...And since the Messenger of Allaah, may Allaah's praise and salutations be upon him, has indicated that the only cure to remove this state of humiliation that we find ourselves entrenched within, is truly returning back to the religion. Then it is clearly obligatory upon us - through the people of knowledge- to correctly and properly understand the religion in a way that conforms to the sources of the Book of Allaah and the Sunnah, and that we educate and raise a new virtuous, righteous generation upon this."

(Clarification and Cultivation and the Need of the Muslims for Them)

It is essential in discussing our perspective upon this obligation of raising the new generation of Muslims, that we highlight and bring attention to a required pillar of these efforts as indicated by Sheikh al-Albaanee, may Allaah have mercy upon him, and others- in the golden words, "*through the people of knowledge*". Since something we commonly experience today is that many people have various incorrect understandings of the role that the scholars should have in the life of a Muslim, failing to understand the way in which they fulfill their position as the inheritors of the Messenger of Allaah, may Allaah's praise and salutations be upon him, and stand as those who preserve and enable us to practice the guidance of Islaam.

Similarly the guiding scholar Sheikh 'Abdul-'Azeez Ibn Baaz, may Allaah have mercy upon him, also emphasized this same overall responsibility:

"...It is also upon a Muslim that he struggles diligently in that which will place his worldly affairs in a good state, just as he must also strive in the correcting of his religious affairs and the affairs of his own family. As the people of his household have a significant right over him that he strive diligently in rectifying their affair and guiding them towards goodness, due to the statement of Allaah, the Most Exalted, ﴾ Oh you who believe! Save yourselves and your families Hellfire whose fuel is men and stones ﴿ -(Surah at-Tahreem: 6)

So it is upon you to strive to correct the affairs of the members of your family. This includes your wife, your children- both male and female- and such as your own brothers. This concerns all of the people in your family, meaning you should strive to teach them the religion, guiding and directing them, and warning them from those matters Allaah has prohibited for us. Because you are the one who is responsible for them as shown in the statement of the Prophet, may Allaah's praise and salutations be upon him, { Every one of you is a guardian, and responsible for what is in his custody. The ruler is a guardian of his subjects and responsible for them; a husband is a guardian of his family and is responsible for it; a lady is a guardian of her husband's house and is responsible for it, and a servant is a guardian of his master's property and is responsible for it....} Then the Messenger of Allaah, may Allaah's praise and salutations be upon him, continued to say, **{...so all of you are guardians and are responsible for those under your authority.}** *(Authentically narrated in Saheeh al-Bukhaaree & Muslim)*

It is upon us to strive diligently in correcting the affairs of the members of our families, from the aspect of purifying their sincerity of intention for Allaah's sake alone in all of their deeds, and ensuring that they truthfully believe in and follow the Messenger of Allaah, may Allaah's praise and salutations be upon him, their fulfilling the prayer and the other obligations which Allaah the Most Exalted has commanded for us, as well as from the direction of distancing them from everything which Allaah has prohibited.

It is upon every single man and women to give advice to their families about the fulfillment of what is obligatory upon them. Certainly, it is upon the woman as well as upon the man to perform this. In this way our homes become corrected and rectified in regard to the most important and essential matters. Allaah said to His Prophet, may Allaah's praise and salutations be upon him, ◈ **And enjoin the ritual prayers on your family...** ◈ *(Surah Taha: 132) Similarly, Allaah the Most Exalted said to His prophet Ismaa'aeel,* ◈ **And mention in the Book, Ismaa'aeel. Verily, he was true to what he promised, and he was a Messenger, and a Prophet. And he used to enjoin on his family and his people the ritual prayers and the obligatory charity, and his Lord was pleased with him.** ◈ *-(Surah Maryam: 54-55)*

As such, it is only proper that we model ourselves after the prophets and the best of people, and be concerned with the state of the members of our households. Do not be neglectful of them, oh worshipper of Allaah! Regardless of whether it is concerning your wife, your mother, father, grandfather, grandmother, your brothers, or your children; it is upon you to strive diligently in correcting their state and condition..."

(Collection of Various Rulings and Statements- Sheikh 'Abdul-'Azeez Ibn 'Abdullah Ibn Baaz, Vol. 6, page 47)

We hope to contribute works which enable every striving Muslim who acknowledges the proper position of the scholars, to fulfill the recognized duty and obligation which lays upon each one of us to bring the light of Islaam into our own lives as individuals as well as into our homes and among our families. Towards this goal we are committed to developing educational publications and comprehensive educational curriculums -through cooperation with and based upon the works of the scholars of Islaam and the students of knowledge. Works which, with the assistance of Allaah, the Most High, we can utilize to educate and instruct ourselves, our families and our communities upon Islaam in both principle and practice. The publications and works of the Nakhlah Educational Series are divided into the following categories:

Basic: Ages 4- 6

Elementary: Ages 6-11

Secondary: Ages 11-14

High School: Ages 14- Young Adult

General: Young Adult –Adult

Supplementary: All Ages

Publications and works within these stated levels will, with the permission of Allaah, encompass different beneficial areas and subjects, and will be offered in every permissible form of media and medium. As certainly, as the guiding scholar Sheikh Saaleh Fauzaan al-Fauzaan, may Allaah preserve him, has stated,

"Beneficial knowledge is itself divided into two categories. Firstly is that knowledge which is tremendous in its benefit, as it benefits in this world and continues to benefit in the Hereafter. This is religious Sharee'ah knowledge. And secondly, that which is limited and restricted to matters related to the life of this world, such as learning the processes of manufacturing various goods. This is a category of knowledge related specifically to worldly affairs.

…As for the learning of worldly knowledge, such as knowledge of manufacturing, then it is legislated upon us collectively to learn whatever the Muslims have a need for. Yet If they do not have a need for this knowledge, then learning it is a neutral matter upon the condition that it does not compete with or displace any areas of Sharee'ah knowledge…"

("Explanations of the Mistakes of Some Writers", Pages 10-12)

We ask Allaah, the most High to bless us with success in contributing to the many efforts of our Muslim brothers and sisters committed to raising themselves as individuals and the next generation of our children upon that Islaam which Allaah has perfected and chosen for us, and which He has enabled the guided Muslims to proceed upon in each and every century. We ask him to forgive us, and forgive the Muslim men and the Muslim women, and to guide all the believers to everything He loves and is pleased with. The success is from Allaah, The Most High The Most Exalted, alone and all praise is due to Him.

Abu Sukhailah Khalil Ibn-Abelahyi
Taalib al-Ilm Educational Resources

30 Days of Guidance [Book 1]: Learning Fundamental Principles of Islaam

A Short Journey Within the Work Al-Ibaanah al-Sughrah With Sheikh 'Abdul-'Azeez Ibn 'Abdullah ar-Raajhee

AUTHOR - COMPILER - TRANSLATOR

Abu Sukhailah Khalil Ibn-Abelahyi

BOOK OVERVIEW

- Interactive course book
- Focused upon both beliefs & principles
- 1st book in 30 Day Series

WHO IS THIS BOOK FOR

All age levels

For every Muslim who wishes to live their life in a way pleasing to Allaah it is essential that they ensure that their beliefs and practices actually have evidence and support from within the sources of Islaam. This work approaches this challenge in a way that allows an individual to proceed through discussions related to this a day at a time over thirty days, based upon explanations from one of today's noble scholars.

WHAT YOU WILL LEARN IN THIS BOOK

Related to essential basic principles of guidance

The role of Islaam in today's world is something which is indisputable and often contested. There are many different understandings of Islaam which range from dangerous extremism, all the way to vulnerable laxity. Yet our well-known scholars continue to work diligently in openly examining and clarifying the false ideas and practices that are attributed to Islaam.

PRICING

PDF PREVIEW

PURCHASE BOOK

- *Hardcover -USD $45.00*
- *Soft cover -USD $27.50*
- *Kindle -USD $09.99*

https://ilm4.us/30daybook1   http://taalib.com/4134

30 Days of Guidance [Book 2]: Cultivating The Character & Behavior of Islaam

A Short Journey Within The Work Al-Adab Al-Mufrad With Sheikh Zayd Ibn Muhammad Ibn Haadee al-Madkhalee

AUTHOR - COMPILER - TRANSLATOR

Abu Sukhailah Khalil Ibn-Abelahyi

BOOK OVERVIEW

- Interactive course book
- Focused upon both character & behavior
- 2nd book in 30 Day Series

WHO IS THIS BOOK FOR

All age levels

This course book is intended for the Muslim individual for self-study, as well as for us as Muslim parents in our essential efforts to educate our children within Islaam and our ongoing endeavor of cultivating them upon the extraordinary character and behavior of our beloved Prophet. It is also intended to be an easy to use classroom resource for our Muslim teachers in the every growing numbers of Islamic centers...

WHAT YOU WILL LEARN IN THIS BOOK

Related to the subject of perfecting ones character

Some of the questions that this course book helps us answer are: Are you prepared for your reckoning? Are you always working for good while you can? Do you remember the benefit in your difficulties? Is your life balanced as was the lives of the Companions? How do you deal with your own faults and those of others? Do you know what things bring you closer to Jannah?....and more

PRICING

- *Hardcover -USD $45.00*
- *Soft cover -USD $27.50*
- *Kindle -USD $09.99*

PDF PREVIEW

https://ilm4.us/30daybook2

PURCHASE BOOK

http://taalib.com/4137

Foundations For The New Muslim & Newly Striving Muslim

A Short Journey through Selected Questions & Answers with Sheikh 'Abdul-'Azeez Ibn 'Abdullah Ibn Baaz

AUTHOR - COMPILER - TRANSLATOR

Abu Sukhailah Khalil Ibn-Abelahyi

BOOK OVERVIEW

- Interactive course book
- Focused upon essential beliefs & challenges
- 4th book in 30 Day Series

WHO IS THIS BOOK FOR

All age levels

This course book is intended for both the person who has newly embraced Islaam or that Muslim or Muslimah whom Allaah has blessed to now have the resolve within themselves to truly turn towards their Most Merciful Lord and commit themselves to becoming a better worshipper upon knowledge. It for that individual who, regardless of the direction they came from, wishes to change both the inward and outward aspects of their lives to now move in a direction truly pleasing to Allaah.

WHAT YOU WILL LEARN IN THIS BOOK

Related to building a firm foundation for our Islaam

This course book discusses What are the conditions of correct Islaam? Is faith only what is in our hearts? When is it necessary for me to ask a scholar? What is the guidance of Islaam about our health? What should I do after falling into sin again and again? Do I have to make up for my previous negligence? How should I interact with the non-Muslims I know? and more...

PRICING

- *Hardcover -USD $45.00*
- *Soft cover -USD $27.50*
- *Kindle -USD $09.99*

PDF PREVIEW

https://ilm4.us/30daybook4

PURCHASE BOOK

http://taalib.com/4147

30 Days of Guidance [Book 3]: Signposts Towards Rectification & Repentance

A Short Journey through Selected Questions & Answers with
Sheikh Muhammad Ibn Saaleh al-'Utheimeen

WHAT YOU WILL LEARN IN THIS BOOK

Related to the Subject of perfecting ones character

This course discusses in detail the inward and outward changes and steps we must take as striving Muslims to improve and bring our lives into a better state after mistakes, sins, slips, and negligence. Discussing real life problems and issues faced by Muslim of all ages and situations -the Sheikh advises and indicates the road to reform, repentance, and true rectification.

AUTHOR - COMPILER - TRANSLATOR

Abu Sukhailah Khalil Ibn-Abelahyi

BOOK OVERVIEW

- Interactive course book
- Focused upon both change & growth in Islaam
- 3rd book in 30 Day Series

WHO IS THIS BOOK FOR

All age levels

This course book is intended for any Muslim who wishes to improve his life and rectify his heart. Yet this self rectification or purification of the soul must be done in the correct way and upon the correct foundation of knowledge from the Sunnah, if it is to lead to true success in both this life and the next. Ibn al-Qayyim, may Allaah have mercy upon him, also stated, 'The true purification of the soul and the self is directly connected to those messengers sent to humanity...'

PRICING

- *Hardcover -USD $45.00*
- *Soft cover -USD $27.50*
- *Kindle -USD $09.99*

PDF PREVIEW

https://ilm4.us/30daybook3

PURCHASE BOOK

http://taalib.com/4150

Statements of the Guiding Scholars of Our Age Regarding Books & their Advice to the Beginner Seeker of Knowledge

[Contains A List of over 300 Books Recommended By The Scholars In The Various Sciences Of Islaam]

AUTHOR - COMPILER - TRANSLATOR

Abu Sukhailah Khalil Ibn-Abelahyi

BOOK OVERVIEW

- Taken from words of senior scholars
- Provides road map for Sharee'ah study
- Divided into seven main sections

WHO IS THIS BOOK FOR

All age levels

A comprehensive guidebook for the Muslim who wishes to learn about his or her religion with the proper goal and aim, in the proper way, and through the proper books. This question and answer book is for those who seek advice from some of the senior scholars of the current century regarding seeking knowledge, against books containing misguidance.

WHAT YOU WILL LEARN IN THIS BOOK

Sources and subjects of seeking Sharee'ah knowledge

This book is intended to enable any sincere Muslim to strive to proceed with correct methods and manners in seeking of beneficial knowledge for themselves and in order to guide their families. The scholars are the carriers of authentic knowledge and the inheritors of the Messenger of Allaah. Their explantations make clear for us the way to learn and then live Islaam.

PRICING

- *Hardcover -USD $45.00*
- *Soft cover -USD $27.50*
- *Kindle -USD $09.99*

PDF PREVIEW

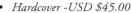
https://ilm4.us/seeker

PURCHASE BOOK

http://taalib.com/79

BOOK PREVIEW

An Educational Course Based Upon Beneficial Answers to Questions On Innovated Methodologies

of Sheikh Saaleh Ibn Fauzaan al-Fauzaan

Abu Sukhailah Khalil Ibn-Abelahyi

BOOK OVERVIEW

- Interactive course book
- Focuses upon principles of the straight path
- Discusses modern groups and movements

WHO IS THIS BOOK FOR

All age levels

This course book is for any Muslim who wishes to understand the detailed guiding principles of Islaam as discussed by the scholars throughout the centuries, including the scholars of our age. These principles were initially put in place and practiced by the generation of the Companions of the Messenger of Allaah, may Allaah be pleased with all of them, when Islaam was first established, and have been implemented in each and every century by those Muslims following in their noble footsteps.

WHAT YOU WILL LEARN IN THIS BOOK

Related to the detailed way we understand Islaam

This course focuses upon the importance of clarity in the way you understand and practice Islaam. What is the right way or methodology to do so? Examine the evidences and proofs from the sources texts of the Qur'aan and Sunnah and the statements of many scholars explaining them, that connect you directly to the Islaam of the Messenger of Allaah.

PRICING

- *Hardcover - USD $50*
- *Soft cover - USD $32.50*
- *Kindle - USD $09.99*

PDF PREVIEW

http://ilm4.us/minhaj

PURCHASE BOOK

http://taalib.com/4144

The Belief of Every Muslim & The Methodology of The Saved Sect

Lessons & Benefits From the Two Excellent Works of Sheikh Muhammad Ibn Jameel Zaynoo

AUTHOR - COMPILER - TRANSLATOR

Abu Sukhailah Khalil Ibn-Abelahyi

BOOK OVERVIEW

* Interactive course book with diagrams
* Discusses how to study and from whom
* Focuses upon both beliefs & practices

WHO IS THIS BOOK FOR

All age levels

This course book is for any Muslim who is looking for an easy-to-follow course- based discussion of not only what it is important to learn but also concise advice on how to study and learn Islaam. Taking selections from two well-known books of Sheikh Zaynoo, may Allaah have mercy upon him, it offers an overview of some of the characteristics and hallmarks which distinguished that clear call our beloved Prophet brought to humanity.

WHAT YOU WILL LEARN IN THIS BOOK

Related to foundation of Islaam & gaining knowledge

This Islamic studies course discusses the different levels of knowledge, important matters related to seeking knowledge, essential study skills, the role of evidence in Islaam, differing and taking from the scholars. Addditionally, it explains the central role that the foundation that worshipping Allaah alone should have in our lives, and how that distinguishes every single person.

PRICING

* *Hardcover -USD $45.00*
* *Soft cover -USD $30*
* *Kindle -USD $09.99*

PDF PREVIEW

https://ilm4.us/savedsect

PURCHASE BOOK

http://taalib.com/4141